Instructor's Guide for

STORY

Fictions Past and Present

Litzinger ⟷ Oates

Robert Luscher
Louisiana State University

Danny Robinson
North Carolina State University at Raleigh

D. C. HEATH AND COMPANY

Lexington, Massachusetts   Toronto

CONTENTS

PART 1

WASHINGTON IRVING

The Legend of
Sleepy Hollow

(p. 1)

By twice removing the narrator from the tale he relates,
Irving contributes to our sense that the adventure at Sleepy
Hollow occurs in the twilight atmosphere between reality
and fantasy. It allows for romantic exaggeration and
speculation. Even the narrator himself believes only half
of his story!
    Like many early American writers, Irving was faced
with the task of making the relatively recent American past
appear romantic and picturesque. Hawthorne, for example,
in his preface to The Marble Faun, noted "the difficulty of
writing a romance about a country where there is no shadow,
no antiquity, no mystery, no picturesque and gloomy wrong,
nor anything but a commonplace prosperity, in broad and
simple daylight." Irving successfully casts an air of
enchantment over the story of the hapless schoolmaster
through his richly descriptive and suggestive style. In
the third paragraph, Irving begins to transform Sleepy
Hollow from a literal to a literary landscape pervaded by a
"drowsy, dreary influence" which causes spells, trances,
visions, superstitions, and "marvellous beliefs." Yet
despite its supernatural elements, the story retains its
characteristically American flavor. Irving is careful
throughout to make full use of the limited history and
tradition which the young nation did possess. He effortlessly
glides from fantasy to folklore to historical anecdote
through repeated references to the American Revolution, the
traditional folkways of the Dutch community, and the
Puritan witchcraft trials. Irving was the first short
story writer to make American settings an integral part of

his tale. Although such tales as "The Legend of Sleepy Hollow" and "Rip Van Winkle" are derived from European folk tales, in Irving's renditions they have become irrevocably associated with the American landscape.

Although not a moralistic tale in the sense of "Young Goodman Brown," "The Legend of Sleepy Hollow" contains keen insights into human nature. Irving's portrait of Ichabod Crane, with his "small shrewdness and simple credulity," his passion for and fear of the romantic and supernatural, is memorable because of its inherent contradictions as well as its comic exaggeration. Crane prides himself on his refinement, on his reputation as a fine dancer and singer, and as a man of great erudition. Yet we see that to his "devouring mind's eye" the wonders of the visible world are chiefly gastronomic ones. Even the object of his heart's affection is viewed by Ichabod as a tempting morsel. Like a true Yankee entrepreneur, Ichabod quickly analyzes how Katrina's rich farmland and orchards "might be readily turned into cash, and the money invested in immense tracts of wild land, and shingle palaces in the wilderness." Ichabod loses Katrina but his various talents and single-mindedness are later rewarded in his rise to a position as justice of the Ten Pound Court.

Other than the dramatic encounter with the headless horseman, very little happens in this tale. It is Irving's skillful storytelling -- his ironic tone and diction and his humorous description -- which makes the story so memorable. His use of American settings, characters, and characteristics marks Irving as a pioneer in the American short story.

HONORÉ DE BALZAC

A Passion in the Desert

Translated by Ellen Marriage

(p. 19)

The opening and closing paragraphs of the story are the
only ones which do not take place in the desert. They
provide a frame for this bizarre tale of the past by
providing a link to present-day society. The opening
paragraphs also provide a firsthand account of the old
soldier whose tale we are about to hear. He is an old,
one-legged warrior with a "frank good-humored expression."
Balzac's description of him as a man of action, one who
"would not hesitate to make friends with the devil himself,"
begins to prepare us for the strange incongruities of his
tale. The menagerie is an appropriate opening setting
since it partakes of both the exotic animal world and
conventional society.

By setting the story far from civilization, Balzac
gives us a momentary illusion that the two protagonists are
free from the restraints of social norms and conventions.
He is able to focus our attention solely on the characters
and their "passion in the desert." We soon see that the
conventions and restraints which they adopt are quite
similar to those of civilized society.

When first contemplating the "immensity" of the desert
and his own solitude, the young soldier loads his rifle and
considers suicide as one means of freeing himself from his
"horrible despair." It is not until he sees some sign of
habitation that the instinct for life returns and he begins
to prepare his camp.

The vivid, realistic description of the soldier's
"profound terror" upon awakening to the panther obscures
the more bizarre fact of the panther's casual acceptance of

her new roommate. The panther is soon seen not as a wild beast but as an object of great power and beauty.

Balzac carefully alters his language in this brief tale to metamorphose the panther from a creature whose savage energy could not belong to a human creature to a beautiful, sensitive feminine being who "has a soul." He begins on a descriptive level using words such as "bracelets," "rings," "dress," "graceful," and "prettiness" that could describe a woman as well as the striking beauty of the panther. The soldier soon begins to interpret her looks and actions in increasingly complex emotional terms. He finds her gracious, affectionate, and even jealous. Ultimately, he feels he knows "the different inflections of her voice, the expressions of her eyes."

The exotic imagery and action of this story are used for emphasis, not for their own sake, as would be the case with a "tall tale." It is a story of passion, which is essentially the same wherever it occurs. The parallels between the passion in the desert and human love are not expressly stated. They are seen, or rather felt, in the ambiguous motives and machinations of the soldier and the panther. Great passions may bring contradictory sentiments -- fear and affection, danger and excitement -- and leave us feeling both more vulnerable and more secure. While "all great passions" need not end in misunderstanding, even a small misunderstanding is likely to have greater consequences in a passionate relationship than in a casual friendship.

The soldier admits that the desert is very beautiful: in some ways it is perfect, "it is God without mankind." Yet he also states he is "not always regretting" his palm trees and panther. The desert, like the panther, like passionate love, represents extreme beauty and extreme danger. There is no middle ground: "there is everything, and nothing."

NATHANIEL HAWTHORNE ====

Young Goodman Brown

(p. 28)

Unlike most symbolic names, Goodman Brown is a rather ordinary, nondescript name. It is ideally suited to the title character, who is not a sharply defined individual but a symbol or representation of all individuals who grow out of an unthinking acceptance of social and religious norms into a realization that the world is a much more complex, and perhaps evil, place than they believed it to be.

Once the "grave" man in the forest is identified as the devil, it becomes clear that the tale is one of Hawthorne's allegories of the human heart, rather than a realistic depiction of early life in Salem. It is no coincidence that the older man bears "considerable resemblance" to the young traveller. Brown's journey into the deepening forest is an allegory of his journey into the moral wilderness of his own nature, once he has left his faith and social sanctions behind him. As in so many of his tales, Hawthorne begins with a literal description and adds numerous romantic and supernatural touches (such as the clouds without wind, the pink ribbons) until we find ourselves in a richly symbolic surrounding. Brown begins on a "dreary road, darkened by all the gloomiest trees," passes on "through the forest, where no church had ever been gathered or solitary Christian prayed," until finally he finds himself "in the heart of the dark wilderness, still rushing onward with the instinct that guides mortal man to evil."

Throughout the tale Hawthorne refrains from describing exactly what happens to Goodman Brown; instead he concentrates on how Brown perceives the events around him. Hawthorne is the master of the ambigous description: the staff "might almost be seen to twist and wriggle itself like a living serpent" but he quickly adds that it "must have been an ocular deception" caused by the uncertain light. Brown sees and hears several similar events throughout his journey, but Hawthorne leaves open the possibility that these are only Brown's subjective interpretations -- perhaps reflecting his subconscious desires -- rather than undisputed facts. This ambiguity is essential to the tale because it leaves the perception and the interpretation of events originally up to Brown and ultimately up to the reader.

On the next morning Goodman Brown is indeed a changed man. Following his "fearful dream" he changes from a relatively naive, innocent young man recently married to his Faith to a "distrustful, if not a desperate man." Whether his journey is only a dream is less important than the fact that his newly discovered awareness of evil marks the turning point in his life. Brown's awareness of the tendency toward evil in his own heart and -- he thinks -- in his fellow man makes it impossible for him to return to his community of his faith in the same spirit in which he left.

Superficially we might see Brown as deceived by his faith and community: the catechism of Goody Cloyse and the Sabbath and lecture day sermons of the old minister do not prepare him for the evil he sees in the forest. On a deeper level, however, Goodman Brown is his own deceiver. It is he, after all, who rejects the supplications of his Faith and insists upon his journey which begins "in such a solitude" and ends "amid calm night and solitude." Even though Brown begins and ends his journey in solitude and self-deception, his primary concern is not with his own evil nature but with the depravity of those around him. His early resistance to the devil is predicated on his assumption that his forefathers and the community elders were God-fearing men. When he realizes this is not the case, he cries "sin is but a name. Come devil; for thee is this world given." Brown's failing is not that he grows out of his early naivete but that he doesn't grow far enough. He learns to look around but not to look within.

NATHANIEL HAWTHORNE

My Kinsman, Major Molineux

(p. 37)

"My Kinsman, Major Molineux" is often read as an initiation story -- one in which Robin undergoes an involuntary rite of passage that changes him from a naive youth to an adult who can make his own way in the world. Although he thinks of himself as a "shrewd" youth, Robin is a country lad completely unprepared for the manners and machinations he is faced with in the town. Instead of being royally welcomed by his kinsman, Robin encounters threats, rejection, and temptation. His first night's experience opens a whole new world of mystery, intrigue, and danger. His confusion increases as the night progresses. At one point he starts suddenly from his reverie of his home life and wonders "Am I here, or there?" But once having entered the adult world, there is no return to the carefree innocence of childhood. His dream ends with the door of his family's house being closed just as he is about to enter. He realizes that he is "excluded from his home." He is left to make his own way in the world without the aid of his kinsman. Robin's provincial origins, inexperience, and reputation for shrewdness -- as yet untested -- encourage many readers to see "My Kinsman, Major Molineux" as an allegory of America's coming-of-age in the eighteenth century, throwing off the British rule and striking out on its own as an independent nation. Just as Robin finds he must "rise in the world" without the assistance of Major Molineux, so too America would be forced to establish itself as a secure, self-sufficient nation without the protection and guidance of Great Britain.

The story is also a useful example of one of Hawthorne's
favorite short story techniques, namely building an entire
story around one central event or revelation which forces
us to re-examine preceding events and discover new significance
in them.

NIKOLAI GOGOL

The Overcoat

Translated by Constance Garnett

(p. 49)

In "The Overcoat" Gogol shows that the common life and perceptions of an average man can supply the material for an interesting and enlightening tale. The ordinary, unexciting, and ostensibly uninteresting activities and feelings of what Frank O'Connor terms "the Little Man" are the source for insight and understanding in the stories of many writers after Gogol. In "A Simple Heart" and "The Death of Ivan Ilych," Flaubert and Tolstoy focus on the activities and ambitions of two rather common individuals, although their morals are very dissimilar. In the twentieth century, Sherwood Anderson and William Faulkner are well known for their use of ordinary events and commonplace characters to reveal fundamental aspects of human nature.

Although he is harsh to Akaky and is, perhaps, the immediate cause of his illness, the Person of Consequence is but representative of the vanity and vulgarity of much of society. The casual callousness of Akaky's fellow clerks, the thieves, and the guards are other examples of the kinds of attitudes which Akaky confronts daily and which encourage him to withdraw into his private world copying documents.

The narrator's comic tone is a means by which he is able to make light, almost whimsical comments which keep us both amused and interested yet do not disguise his serious observations on society. Such a comic approach allows him to exaggerate Akaky's qualities, as well as those of the other clerks and the Person of Consequence. As in a cartoon sketch, the narrator presents his keen analysis of human nature under the guise of caricature.

Students may see the overcoat as a symbol of several
changes in Akaky's life or of needs and desires which were
previously unexpressed. The narrator tells us that the
very idea of the overcoat gives Akaky "spiritual nourishment":
"His whole existence had in a sense become fuller, as
though he had married." The overcoat gives Akaky a momentary
sense of self-esteem and serves as a link connecting him
with much of the everyday world from which he had long
secluded himself.

EDGAR ALLAN POE

The Fall of the House of Usher

(p. 67)

Roderick Usher's extreme sensitivity, what the narrator
terms his "morbid acuteness of the senses," is the central
subject of the tale. It is the outward sign of what Darryl
Abel has called Usher's "psychic disintegration." The
epigraph implies that Usher has little or no control over
his responses. As the story progresses, Usher appears to
have become disembodied sensibility. Over the years he has
gradually retired from the outside world, to the point of
not leaving his mansion for many years. It is appropriate
that the epigraph is taken from Béranger's poem "Le Refus,"
which might be translated as "The Denial."

Much of the power of Poe's tale comes from the fact
that the narrator is both fascinated by Usher's rapid
decline and powerless to avert it. Not only does he fail
in his attempts to restore Usher to some semblance of
rationality, but the narrator finds that his own power of
reason is slowly giving way to his friend's "phantasmagoric
conceptions." After Madeline is in the tomb, the narrator
can no longer easily explain his own feelings. Indeed, he
finds he must struggle "to reason off the nervousness"
which is beginning to have "dominion" over him.

Poe carefully selects his titles, both real and
imaginary, for their exotic qualities. The real works
mentioned are all concerned with the fantastic, the
supernatural, or some branch of pseudo-science such as
chiromancy, or alchemy. Poe's own contributions, "The
Haunted Palace," and The Mad Tryst, are works that exploit
the romantic and gothic literary conventions which were very
popular throughout the first half of the nineteenth century.

11

(Students might be interested to know that interest in the romantic past reached such a degree that in England some wealthy land owners actually had ruins <u>built</u> on their estates!)

Poe leaves open the possibility of being buried alive -- a favorite gothic literary convention -- by describing Madeleine's malady early in the story as "of a partially cataleptical character." Conceivably, a person with catalepsy could become extremely rigid, fail to respond to external stimuli, and be mistaken for one already dead. Madeleine's withdrawal and "living death" prefigure that of her twin brother, with whom she has always had an especially close, albeit mysteriously defined, relationship.

Poe's theory that a short story should possess "unity of effect" is nowhere more clearly demonstrated than in the eerie, surreal atmosphere that he creates in this tale. There is very little action or characterization. Although ostensibly about Usher's decline, the tale is actually a study in the artist's ability to create an effect -- of foreboding or of an unnamed terror -- by use of language. Poe chooses his descriptive words for what they suggest as well as what they say, for their sound as well as their meaning. (Ask students to read the first few sentences or the last paragraph aloud to emphasize this quality.) The narrator, for example, often suggests or hints at his meaning or perception rather than stating it outright. He repeatedly regrets that only a fraction of his intense experience can be "shadowed forth" in "merely written words." Through such techniques Poe forces us both to participate in the events and to intensify them.

The story would have to occur in the old world, where the gothic conventions of decay, mysterious ancient chambers, tombs, old "time-honored" races, and "peasantry" are more easily accounted for. As with most such romantic, gothic tales, any actual setting is but a pale reflection of the rich, exotic world of the artist's imagination.

We are informed early in the tale that the peasants associate the House of Usher with both the family and the mansion itself. It appears set off from the rest of the landscape, much as Usher himself is isolated from society. The more we learn about Usher's diseased state of the mind, the more the decaying old structure appears to be an appropriate reflection of its owner. By the end of the tale, however, we may come to view the house as symbolic of

the nonrational, unexplained -- and perhaps unexplainable --
side of the human psyche. The mystery and terror of the old
mansion may reflect the mystery and fear within Roderick
Usher and within the reader as well.

EDGAR ALLAN POE

The Cask of Amontillado

(p. 79)

The opening sentence not only gives us the history of the
narrator's relationship with Fortunato, but tells us a good
deal about Montresor himself. Superficially, he is a "man
of honor" who can bear injury but not insult. Significantly,
however, Montresor does not return the insult or challenge
Fortunato openly, but instead vows a surreptitious revenge.

The narrator has a keen sense of human nature in
general and of Fortunato in particular. He knows that the
very characteristics which make Fortunato "respected and
even feared" can be manipulated to bring about his destruction.
Fortunato's weak point is not his love of wine but his
pride in connoisseurship. His pride makes him self-confident
and reckless. He insults the narrator, refers to Luchesi as
an "ignoramus," and insists on sampling the Amontillado
personally. The narrator manipulates both his servants and
Fortunato through reverse psychology. Montresor is deceitful
but deadly serious. His character is not so much "developed"
as it is "revealed," both through his actions and his irony.

Students might associate the Italian Carnival with the
American Mardi Gras. The revelry, bizarre costumes, dancing,
and celebration provide a time and atmosphere in which one
can lay aside his or her conventional role or demeanor and
assume, for a brief period, a new identity. Fortunato,
drunk with wine and the excitement of the carnival, is
caught off guard; Montresor takes advantage of the social
chaos during "the supreme madness of the carnival season"
to accomplish his covert plan.

Montresor's coat of arms, with the foot crushing the
serpent whose fangs are imbedded in the heel, might be seen

14

as a fitting picture for the story as a whole. Fortunato
is a powerful man, both respected and feared, whom the
narrator does not dare to insult publicly. Yet the narrator
knows his enemy's weakness, his Achilles heel, and consequently
is able to destroy a rival capable of crushing him.

Montresor is in earnest. When he encounters Fortunato
during the carnival he can scarcely believe in his good
fortune. His cautions about Fortunato's other engagements
and his health only serve to make his enemy more reckless.
Montresor is a master of irony and doubtless enjoys his
double-entendres both for his own pleasure and for the
effect they will later have on Fortunato. As Montresor
notes in the first paragraph of his tale, a wrong is
unredressed when "the avenger fails to make himself felt as
such to him who has done the wrong."

Montresor's final words are ambiguous; they may be
ironic. On the other hand, the murder took place over a
half century before, and, since retribution has not overtaken
Montresor, he may feel that he has had his revenge. The
words may also be taken literally. Montresor may not yet
be ready to have his deed discovered and would just as soon
have Fortunato's remains undisturbed.

EDGAR ALLAN POE

The Purloined Letter

(p. 84)

At first glance, the plot of this tale appears to be less
unified than those of "The Fall of the House of Usher" and
"The Cask of Amontillado." The swift-paced action of the
first half of the story, culminates in Dupin's long-winded,
although interesting, account of human reasoning. A
detective story depends on suspense for much of its interest.
By postponing the final scene with its minute description
of how Dupin outwitted his adversary, Poe is able to increase
our suspense by forcing us to wait and speculate.

Minister D------ is, of course, Dupin's adversary in
his attempts to regain the purloined letter. In many ways,
however, these two old acquaintances are very similar.
Both are poets as well as men of reason and cunning. Unlike
the Prefect, the minister and the detective are imaginative
individuals, as well as bold men of action who give the
appearance of ennui. In some respects, then, Dupin's
antagonist is not the minister so much as it is the generally
accepted ways of thinking and feeling represented by the
Prefect.

Dupin describes the Parisian police as "persevering,
ingenious, cunning." Their cunning, however, is not that
of the sly fox or of the thief who lives by his wits. It
is an unimaginative thoroughness, what Dupin calls the
"jealous scrutiny of the microscope." The "good sense" of
men like Dupin -- and the minister -- stems from the fact
that their perceptions are both more profound and more
simple than those of the industrious Prefect.

Poe is often acknowledged as the originator of the
modern short detective story. "The Purloined Letter"

demonstrates his mastery of its techniques. Although the
letter is discovered midway through the tale, Poe manages
to hold us in suspense as he slowly unravels how the mystery
was solved. The point of view is crucial to the story's
overall effect. Much of the surprise and suspense derive
from the fact that we are given the facts of the case in
the same order in which they were revealed to the narrator.
The unexpected appearance of the Prefect, the surprising
appearance of the letter in Dupin's desk, and the revelation
of how the mystery was solved would be less effective if
told from a different point of view. The use of a narrator
also allows Poe to keep the character of Dupin somewhat
mysterious: we see his results and hear his theory long
before we see him in action.

The narrator -- like Dr. Watson for Sherlock Holmes in
Conan Doyle's "The Red-Headed League" -- serves as a foil
for Dupin, providing a perspective with which the reader can
identify. Both Poe's narrator and Dr. Watson, although
personally close to the protagonist, remain essentially
outsiders observing the movements and deliberations of a
master sleuth. Dr. Watson, in that he participates more
directly in the action, has an advantage over the narrator
of "The Purloined Letter." To most readers, likewise,
Holmes appears more vivid than Dupin. Holmes is seen in a
greater variety of settings -- in conversation, at a concert,
in pursuit of his investigations -- than is Dupin. Conan
Doyle also endows Sherlock Holmes with a number of memorable
personal traits. Dupin, on the other hand, remains primarily
a theorist -- the prototype of the detective, of which
Holmes is a highly individualized example.

HERMAN MELVILLE

Bartleby the Scrivener

A Story of Wall-Street

(p. 97)

The subtitle, "A Story of Wall-Street," is significant
because it underscores several of the story's central
themes. It would be too simple to suggest that "Bartleby"
is simply an indictment of American commercial life;
Melville's scope is much broader. His story is an indictment
of our tendency, reflected and reinforced by our commercial
society, to value the outward signs of success over more
personal values and ideals. America has so taken to heart
Benjamin Franklin's ideal of industry and frugality that
there is no place for one like Bartleby except among the
"murderers and thieves" of a prison. Although the narrator
is not a cruel or unfeeling man, his first loyalty is to
his position as a respectable businessman. He prides
himself on his personal association with John Jacob Astor
and admits that he enjoys repeating the name which "rings
like unto bullion." It is no coincidence that when the
narrator comes to hear a "celebrated preacher" the church
is located in the Wall Street district. He knows that
Bartleby is "harmless" but the "unsolicited and uncharitable
remarks" of his business associates result in his decision
to leave Bartleby to fend for himself. Despite his compassion
for the unaggressive scrivener, the narrator writes that he
simply cannot tolerate the idea of Bartleby "denying my
authority, and perplexing my visitors and scandalizing my
professional reputation."

Students should be encouraged to discuss the extent to
which the narrator, and the value system he represents, is
responsible for Bartleby's condition. Although he is
distressed when he sees Bartleby behind prison walls, the

narrator fails to see that the working conditions he set up for Bartleby in the office were even more confining. He placed Bartleby between a window which "commanded no view at all" save that of a building wall three feet away and "a high green folding screen which might entirely isolate" the copyist from all others in the office. This physical isolation emphasizes Bartleby's emotional detachment. We are never explicitly told the reasons for the scrivener's usual behavior, yet we have some clue simply by thinking of the impersonal, mechanical nature of his profession. Nothing is required of Bartleby other than an unimaginative attention to detail. His human qualities would only interfere with his tasks. The narrator reinforces this opinion through his habit of calling Bartleby to his desk and handing him documents to copy without even looking up from the original. Turkey and Nippers escape from such a mindless routine through alcohol and radical personality changes. Bartleby withdraws into a passive isolation beyond the reach of the narrator's cajoling, bribes, or threats. The narrator is disconcerted and annoyed but Bartleby's extreme passivity has a disarming effect on him. He refuses to take strong action against Bartleby -- until he realizes that his reputation is in jeopardy. It speaks well of the narrator that despite his exclamations that "Bartleby was nothing to me," he does feel compassion for his clerk and tries to do what he can for him. Nevertheless, the narrator never seriously questions his own social and personal values which, magnified on a societal scale, may be partly responsible for Bartleby's behavior. He prefers not to.

FYODOR DOSTOEVSKY

The Grand Inquisitor

Translated by Constance Garnett

(p. 120)

By setting the story of Christ and the Inquisitor within
the framework of the relationship between the two brothers,
Dostoevsky is able to emphasize its themes by noting how
differently Alyosha and Ivan regard the tale. The tension
between the two brothers results from diffrent world views
which, in some ways, are similar to the different views of
man held by the Inquisitor and his captive. Aloysha resists
the true significance of the story. He says he doesn't
understand, asks for clarification, and finally calls the
whole story absurd. He seems to feel he has dismissed the
import of the story when he tells his brother, "Your suffering
inquisitor is a mere fantasy." But Ivan doesn't mind this
appellation. "Of course it's a fantasy," he replies. He is
less concerned with literal than imaginative truth. Aloysha,
however, is more pragmatic than imaginative; he is more
interested in fact than truth. The striking difference
between the brothers complements the conflict of the central
story.

   The inquisitor has Christ arrested because he knows
that His presence will have a disturbing effect on the
masses. The Inquisitor and his predecessors have begun to
persuade the people to give up their freedom -- indeed to
loathe it -- and accept security and material comfort in
its stead. Christ's appearance will remind people that
there are ideals which are more important than bread, that
men have power and responsibility to choose between good
and evil, that the burden of freedom is what makes man
different from the rest of creation. The Inquisitor is not
interested in ideals or faith. He is a practical, and in

many ways, a shrewd man who knows the weaknesses of human nature. "Feed men, and then ask of them virtue," he tells Christ (a statement which echoes Benjamin Franklin's maxim in Poor Richard's Almanac: "It is hard for an empty sack to stand upright").

Dostoevsky is able to make Christ a powerful figure by contrasting his silence and passivity with the Inquisitor's heated argument. Christ does not answer the Inquisitor because such an issue cannot be resolved through debate. The Inquisitor is right about man's desire for certainty and his weakness for mystery and miracle. But Christ did not come to earth to establish a convenient religion, one suited to human foibles. The Inquisitor's vision is logical and practical perhaps, but is not ennobling. He has, in Coleridge's words, embraced the love of wisdom over the wisdom of love. Christ's kiss at the end of the old man's bitter harangue says more than words could say about what is lacking in the Cardinal's philosophy. The love, forgiveness, and compassion represented by the kiss are nowhere to be found in the Inquisitor's vision of society.

GUSTAVE FLAUBERT ═══════════

A Simple Heart

Translated by Arthur McDowall

(p. 132)

A useful exercise is to ask students to look up "simple" in an unabridged dictionary. Flaubert uses many of its meanings to describe Félicité's habits and character: "not compounded or complex; easy to understand; plain; without guile or deceit; innocent, artless; without ostentation or affectation; unpretending; natural; of a low rank or position; common, ordinary." (Webster's New World Dictionary of the American Language) Her simplicity keeps her world narrow but it also keeps her attention focused on the most important things in life, on human and divine love. The simplicity which appears to be a handicap at the beginning of the story is the source of her strength by the end.

It is not what happens to Félicité but how she perceives what happens to her and those she loves which reveals her nature. The close encounter with the charging bull would have made an exciting, heroic tale if it had happened to another. But Félicité "did not pride herself on it" and had no "suspicion that she had done anything heroic." She is devoted to others, especially Virginie, Paul, and Victor, and appears to take more pleasure in their success and happiness than her own. Her intense emotional response to Virginie's first communion reflects this quality: "with the imaginativeness of deep and tender feeling it seemed to her that she actually was the child." In contrast, Félicité's own communion the next morning "did not give her the same exquisite delight."

The painted window, like the colorful parrot later in the story, is symbolic to Félicité of the beauty and comfort of her religion. Flaubert tells us that she understood nothing of doctrines -- nor did she try. The story of the Passion and the symbols of the church were enough to fill her "simple" heart. The final scene, with church-wardens, singers, and children kneeling in silence and the religious festival surrounding her, emphasize those things most important in her life: her religious faith and her love for others.

The subject of the story is the character of Félicité, not her adventures. It is not the action so much as the simple, direct manner of its presentation that reveals her essential traits of devotion, sympathy, and faith to us. Although the story begins by noting that "Félicité was the envy of the ladies of Pont-l'Eveque for half a century," few of the people she loves and serves have any real appreciation of her. Her first employers treat her cruelly, her young man abandons her for a secure life with an older woman, and Madame Aubain generally treats her as a simpleton and takes for granted her sympathy and dedication. Even the children, who are the object of much of her energy and concern, show little evidence of appreciating her. Victor takes advantage of her good nature, Virginie soon becomes too old to be call "thou," and Paul, after his mother's death, sells the furnishings and puts the house up for sale with no thought of the woman who had cared for him as a child.

At the end of "The Red-Headed League" (p. 334) Holmes quotes Flaubert's letter to George Sand: "L'homme c'est rien -- l'oeuvre c'est tout" (the man is nothing -- the work is everything). With her simple heart, her humility and devotion, and her religious faith, Félicité embodies this concept. Although her work consists of the most mundane chores, she performs it diligently without thought of praise or material gain. It is her love, not the hope of worldly success or comfort, which sustains her.

LEO TOLSTOY

The Death of Ivan Ilych

Translated by Louise and Aylmer Maude

(p. 152)

The story of Ivan Ilych is a fictional exploration of
Thoreau's maxim that the unexamined life is not worth
living. In a sense, Ivan does not really begin to live
until he begins to die. Only after his fall does Ivan
begin to think and feel as an individual and not as a member
of his social circle. Only then does he realize that his
lifestyle, professional demeanor, and even his morals were
dictated by others. In his singleminded quest for success
and respectability Ivan paid little attention to the need
for personal convictions and self-respect. Just as his
physical dissipation is emblematic of his spiritual poverty,
so too is his isolation during his illness representative
of a lifelong isolation. (This isolation is what distinguishes
Ivan's simple life from that of Félicité in "A Simple
Heart," who lived a deeply spiritual, deeply emotional
life.) Though Ivan's public and private life was thoroughly
"correct," he lacked any vital relation to his family or to
the ethics of his profession. His domestic relations
mirrored his professional activities in which he would
reduce a complicated emotional case to "its externals,
completely excluding his personal opinion of the matter
while above all observing every prescribed formality."
    Tolstoy begins with Ivan's death and the reactions it
stirred among his wife and his associates. His widow
appears less interested in his passing than in his pension.
Similarly, although he was liked by all of his colleagues
their first thoughts were not of Ivan or their personal
loss but of "the changes and promotions [his death] would
occasion among themselves or their acquaintance." By

24

beginning in this manner with Ivan's death, Tolstoy establishes
a context within which to evaluate his life. In light of
his ultimate end, Ivan's values and lifestyle appear
especially pitiful. Our awareness of Ivan's death allows
us to view the story of his life with some ironic detachment.
Such sentences as "on the whole Ivan Ilych's life continued
to flow as he considered it should -- pleasantly and
properly" can be read ironically in the light of his eventual
isolation and death. Ivan's life-long emphasis on respectability, propriety, formality and good breeding do not
sustain him during his last days. Only then does he question
whether he has lived as he ought. He is able to see much
of himself in the unfeeling solicitations of his wife and
the cool, impersonal professionalism of his doctor. We
recall that Ivan, too, had previously prided himself in his
ability to "separate his real life from the official side
of affairs." Once he has confronted the truth concerning
his past life, once he is able to appreciate and respect
the honesty and simplicity of his servant Gerasim, Ivan is
able to face his death without fear. His pain remains but
his agony is over. Death itself is less dreadful than the
fear of death, which is perhaps especially strong in those
who have lived the unexamined life.

MARK TWAIN
(SAMUEL L. CLEMENS)

The Celebrated Jumping Frog
of Calaveras County

(p. 187)

Twain's celebrated story is most often remembered as the
source of the tale referred to in its title, but the humorous
anecdote about Smiley and Dan'l Webster is but one part of
this masterful exposé of storytelling as a deceptive art.
The first, unnamed narrator, who has connections with the
East, might be seen as a writer in search of Western material
for his stories, not unlike Twain himself. His motives for
relating a tale which he admits from the beginning he found
"as tedious as it should be useless to me" should be suspect.
Just as Wheeler backs him "into a corner and blockaded me
there with his chair," he will more subtly maneuver his
reader into position. By undercutting Wheeler as a
storyteller and disclaiming responsibility for its
implausibility and seeming trivial content, the narrator
may simultaneously take credit for any pleasing results as
a function of his re-telling of the story. Outside both
these narrators stands Twain himself, indulgently laughing
with Simon Wheeler at the narrator's gullibility and subtly
exposing the pretenses of both storytellers.

Wheeler's tale is a rambling monologue, full of
exaggeration and comic comparisons to entertain his listener
as he engages in his deception. Although he was asked about
the Rev. Leonidas Smiley, Wheeler embarks on a narrative
about Jim Smiley, a decidely non-clerical gambler with a
consuming passion for betting. In Wheeler's hands, Smiley
becomes a larger-than-life caricature of a stock Western
figure. Each of the successive beast fables in the narrative
re-runs an ancient story in a Western context and builds up
Smiley's obsession in preparation for the climax. The mare

and the bull-pup both illustrate some human quality, but
Dan'l Webster is the most personified of the three. Educable
and "gifted," he is designed to elicit our sympathy almost
as if he were a human contestant.

While we might sympathize with Dan'l as the victim of
the stranger's cruelty, there is some delight in seeing
Smiley beaten at his own game. Perhaps the tall tale
becomes less plausible as Wheeler exaggerates the "facts"
of his narrative, but we read on for pleasure of watching
the trickster tricked. The frame of Twain's story provides
a similar pleasure, as we watch the narrator conned by
Simon Wheeler, who senses that he is a ready audience for
his rambling and exaggerated anecdote. As the narrator
flees from Wheeler at the conclusion, we too suspect that
the narrator has been engaging our attention by some ruse,
but nonetheless excuse the deception for the diversion the
language, characters, and narrative structure have provided.

AMBROSE BIERCE

Moxon's Master

(p. 192)

Although this story has some elements of a nineteenth-century science fiction tale, Bierce's emphasis is less on science or character than on the idea of man's relation to his creations. Bierce prepares us for the appearance of a thinking machine by beginning with definitions, moving on to the example of plant life, and referring finally to the "intelligent cooperation among the constituent elements of the crystals." Moxon concludes that "all matter is sentient." While the narrator disagrees, he nevertheless begins to refer to the machine as if it were human. "Some person," he terms it, and even assigns it the female gender.

Characterization plays a subservient role to Bierce's thematic concerns. Neither the narrator nor the inventor is a well-developed character. Moxon in particular is described as too logical, and even mechanical, in his responses. Bierce is implying there may be dangers in becoming too theoretical, too far removed from everyday life and conventions.

Haley's "answer" to the narrator's last question pulls us sharply back into the world of reality, of commonly accepted ways of thinking and feeling. We begin to realize, as does the narrator in the last paragraph, that what he "saw" would not be accepted as fact. With Moxon dead, the only other remaining participant is Haley, who remains a rather uncommunicative and mysterious phenomenon.

HENRY JAMES

Four Meetings

(p. 199)

James's narrator is a sophisticated, mannered observer,
versed in both the American and European cultures and able
to function easily in either realm. He exhibits a strong
sense of control -- both in his narration and in the
situations as he depicts them within that narration. When
he first meets Caroline Spencer, he fuels her naive enthusiasm
for Europe with his commentary on its charms. The experienced
narrator appears to have some perspective on the American
obsession with Europe, yet he concludes his analysis of the
"great American disease" with the observation that what a
European journey does "is merely to confirm and consecrate
our confident dream." In his treatment of Caroline's
inflated expectations as "harmless comedy," the narrator
reveals his unawareness of the extent to which these dreams
dominate her life and promote "a kind of craziness."
        After less than a day in Europe, Miss Spencer falls
prey to her Europeanized cousin, whose Byronic pose and
story of misfortune are transparent to the narrator's
seasoned eye. The cousin seemingly dares the narrator to
expose him, but the narrator remains noncommital, watching
instead of acting. For Caroline, the ordinary seaport of
Le Havre, her cousin, and his "countess" provide all the
tangible Europe she needs because she is "lost in the vision
and imagination of everything." While her gullibility and
her dream vision of Europe cloud her perception, some of the
blame for her victimization must rest on the narrator as
well at this juncture for his failure to alert her to the
true nature of her shifty-eyed cousin. While the narrator
does attempt to tell Miss Spencer that she has been swindled

after the fact, he cannot overcome her strong illusions about "old-world romance," which are all that remain after her cousin has taken her savings as he does the flesh from the apricot at his breakfast.

"Madame la Comtesse," the cousin's European counterpart, likewise assumes a role in which Caroline is all too eager to cast her. Although she attempts to put on the airs of a countess when she comes to stay with Miss Spencer, her imposture is immediately obvious to the narrator. He recognizes that her manners are "course, common, affected" and that her story about her Provencal ancestry is false. The fact that she even permits the obsequious attentions of Mr. Mixter should indicate that the Countess has no real claim to the title to which she pretends. Mixter, ostensibly her pupil in French, glorifies her "Europeanness" even more than Miss Spencer once did; the Countess sees him as "stupidity personified" but is willing to take his money for French lessons that are lost on her suitor. Although Caroline has become little more that a waiting maid, she seems to recognize that her permanent house guest does not represent Europe as she once dreamed of it; she may also be aware of her imposture.

The narrator's final lines are highly ironic; he cruelly recognizes that Miss Spencer's initial wish to "see something of dear old Europe" will now be fulfilled for perhaps the rest of her life. Yet the Countess remains her only tie to Europe -- the only memento of an abortive journey. Rather than reminding Caroline of her disappointment, the Countess's presence keeps her fragile dreams from crumbling altogether. The narrator dispassionately examines and courteously participates in her desperate attempt to uphold her illusions at the conclusion, but with no awareness of his role in this drama, which to him is simply "four meetings." After reading the story, students should be encouraged to re-examine the noncommital, self-justifying tone of the narrator's initial remarks and to attempt to supply the word he leaves out of the first paragraph.

Brooksmith

(p. 219)

As in many of his stories, such as the other two in this
anthology, James is concerned with the manners and morals
of a small class in society, members of which are defined
by their refinement, intelligence, and sensitivity. The
narrator's French phrases, like his interest in the "famous
institution of the salon," which he terms the "finest flower
of social life," help to establish his membership in what
he terms "the casual class," and set the tone of worldly
sophistication. Although the narrator is slow to realize
it, Mr. Offord is aware that Brooksmith is more than simply
a butler. He is a participant, one who enjoys "mingling in
the conversation" even though he never says a word. In his
other jobs Brooksmith finds not only that he is not encouraged
to take an interest, but that there is little life -- little
vital, imaginative life -- to participate in. He finds
none of that "criticism of life" which was the essence of
Mr. Offord's salon.

    In explanation of his failure to take Brooksmith into
his employment, the narrator tells us that he couldn't then
have afforded to "keep a man" for his two-room apartment.
But he goes on to suggest that even if his circumstances
were different, his relationship with Brooksmith was such
that he wouldn't have ventured to broach the idea himself.
Indeed, the butler's attitude and manner, correct yet
intimate, leave the narrator with an "odd mixture of
feelings." Although he does not agree that Brooksmith is
"spoiled," neither does he know how Brooksmith will adapt
from being Mr. Offord's" most intimate friend" to the status
of mere servant.

Students may differ as to whether Brooksmith is a snob
-- for which there is abundant evidence -- or whether he
is, as the narrator terms him, "an artist," with a natural
sense of proportion and refinement. The narrator is able
to draw a very fine line between the two. The butler has a
high ideal of what his employer's society should include,
both in his guests and his servants. Indeed, we are told
that if Brooksmith had been Mr. Offord he "certainly would
have found Brooksmith wanting." It may be more than mere
snobbery, however, when the butler finds his later employers
"vulgar" and "dull," just as soap operas appear dull to one
used to Shakespeare.

Superficially, Brooksmith has been spoiled by the
freedom Mr. Offord granted him in running the salon and in
taking him into his confidence as a friend. More importantly,
in being exposed to the world of refinement and imagination
Brooksmith has become ill-suited for his station: "society
had become a neccessity of Brooksmith's nature." Not the
society of wealth but that of ideas, of "reciprocity," has
awakened a spiritual longing in the butler which, as he
correctly prophesies, he is unable to find elsewhere.

HENRY JAMES

The Beast in the Jungle

(p. 229)

Henry James, together with William Dean Howells, was a
leading spokesman for the realist school of fiction.
Realist writers sought to avoid many of the conventions of
their Romantic predecessors. They shunned the romantic
concepts of the sublime and the beautiful in favor of the
more common, if less extreme, experiences of people in
general. The romantic hero was replaced by a more ambivalent,
less idealized counterpart. "The Beast in the Jungle" is
one of James's most powerful indictments of the dangers of
the romantic sensibility. Marcher's obsession with something
"rare and strange, possibly prodigious and terrible" that
may happen to him reveals his Romantic outlook. He ignores
the pleasures and struggle of ordinary life in order to
devote all of his energies to waiting for his idealized,
though amorphous vision to come to pass. Even human love
is of little consequence in comparison to Marcher's grandiose
expectations. How little he values it is indicated by his
answer to May's early suggestion that the "something"
awaited may be the "sense of danger, familiar to so many
people -- of falling in love." Marcher's flippant response
that "of course what's in store for me may be no more than
that" prefigures his isolation and reveals the high price
he's paid for living with his illusions.
   James portrays the Romantic sensiblity as essentially
selfish and self-centered. Marcher's actions and feelings
reveal him as very different from his self-image. He enjoys
thinking of himself as "the most harmless of maniacs,"
describes his attitude as "heroic" and regards himself as
"sublimely-unselfish." Yet he is unable to set aside his own

concerns even momentarily. May escapes Marcher's fate through her love for him. She lets her association with him "give shape and colour to her own existence." Not until the end, however, does Marcher realize that he has thought of her only "in the chill of his egotism and the light of her use." Marcher's capacity for self-deception is suggested in the story's opening scene. Despite Marcher's claims to the contrary, May Bartram realizes that Marcher "really didn't remember the least thing about her." He sees her not as a separate individual but simply as an episode in his own life. Her face was "a reminder yet not quite a remembrance."

This story is an excellent study in the art of foreshadowing. The first paragraphs suggest all of what we later discover to be Marcher's true nature: his vanity, his illusions, his peculiar blindness. Seemingly simple phrases or descriptions become more meaningful when reread in the light of the final revelations. In the second paragraph, for example, we read that May "hadn't lost it, but she wouldn't give it back to him ... without some putting forth of his hand for it." Similarily, Marcher's early pride in being "the most disinterested person in the world" would come back to haunt him.

Some students may not detect such foreshadowing and be disappointed that the final revelation is not something unusual but rather what we should have expected all along. Like Marcher, they may be victims of a Romantic sensibility which ignores elemental passions in favor of "something" mysterious or exotic.

SARAH ORNE JEWETT

Miss Tempy's Watchers

(p. 256)

In this simple story, as in many of her tales, Jewett
examines the traits and celebrates the virtues of the men
and women of rural New England. She is interested less in
action than in revealing the character of those who have
struggled against and adapted to the harsh realities of the
land. The close attention to specific mannerisms, dialect,
and social attitudes gives her tales a vivid New England flavor.

    The background information on Mrs. Crowe and Miss
Binson sets the stage for what follows. It introduces the
two women and gives us some perspective by which we can
evaluate their actions and conversation. Both childless,
both friends of Miss Tempy, both "dry, shrewd, quick witted,"
the women nevertheless represent two extremes within the
community, in both temperament and circumstances. Mrs.
Crowe has a "cooler disposition" than Miss Binson and though
she "looked kindly" she is not as generous as her neighbor.
Miss Binson's poverty and heavy responsibilities have taken
their toll on her "sharp-set" countenance.

    Their conversation reveals their attitudes on such
different topics as children, generosity, and death. It
also tells us a great deal about Miss Tempy herself. By
describing Mrs. Crowe's guilty feelings or Miss Binson's
humility and loyalty, the author gives us a perspective
from which to evaluate Miss Tempy's life and character. We
learn of her compassion for children, her generosity, her
excellent preserves, her "unused best room," her "young
heart," her kindness to her friends. Even in death Miss
Tempy acts as a liaison between these two "oldest friends,"
who once had come "near to hard feelings." The long

35

vigil has its effect on the two women, especially on Mrs. Crowe, who comes to appreciate the thoughtfulness of Sister Binson. Miss Tempy's hope that they might become closer during their long secluded night together is partly realized. Each, we are told, "had already told the other more than one fact that she had determined to keep secret." Even after her death Miss Tempy is able to do with her friends what she did with her quince-tree: "tend to it, and look at it so pleasant, and kind of expect the old thorny thing into bloomin'."

Miss Tempy not only gives Mrs. Crowe a "new sympathy" for her fellow townswomen but also serves as an example of generosity and provides an opportunity for her friend to gain a better understanding of death. Previously both women had "dreaded the great change." The vigil stirs the sympathies of both women, yet they cannot escape the feeling that they are being watched. The author suggests that the friends' new feeling may be apparent to the deceased woman, that perhaps Miss Tempy herself "was the only watcher."

Désirée's Baby

(p. 263)

The French and Indian influence in southern Louisiana
created a very different social and cultural environment
from that of the typical white/black communities of most of
the antebellum South. Chopin's use of French titles and
expressions distinguishes her setting -- a setting which
makes the events of her story much more plausible. The
frequent mixture of blacks, whites, Creoles, and Cajuns in
southern Louisiana, especially New Orleans, makes it much
more likely that a foundling such as Désirée might have
mixed ancestry. There are also small hints that Armand may
not be white. His face is described as "dark" and Désirée
points out that his skin is darker than hers.

The fact that we do not see his mother, who is French
and not a Southern white, leaves open the possibility that
Armand may not be what he appears. His treatment of the
slaves, far more severe than his father's, becomes even
harsher after he learns that his baby is not white. The
baby might be seen as a confirmation of something which
Armand cannot accept about himself.

Armand's character remains consistent throughout. He
is a passionate man. He falls in love at first sight; he
is very proud of the Aubigny name; and, at first, he is
"the proudest father in the parish." His bitterness, his
sense of betrayal, is equally passionate. He cannot excuse
the "unconscious injury she had brought upon his home and
his name." He sends away his wife and baby rather than
have a stain on his family name. Because Désirée is a
foundling, she is easy prey to his "explanation" of why the
baby resembles the quadroon slave. Although they love her

37

and want her to come home, Désirée's parents do not dispute Armand's accusation. She is no match for her husband's strong nature and, indeed, may even have come to believe he is right.

The story is one about parental love, as well as the shaping force of social prejudice. We see Désirée's love for her baby, Madame Valmondé's love for Désirée, and, in the final paragraph, Armand's mother's love for him. By rejecting his family in order to save his family name, Armand clearly stands apart from the women in the story, an example of the high price of social position and prejudice.

JOSEPH CONRAD

Heart of Darkness

(p. 268)

Written in 1902, "Heart of Darkness" questions the fundamental
precepts of British colonial rule. Marlow begins his journey
with a casual acceptance of the white man's burden to bring
"civilization" -- the religion, laws, morality, and culture
of Europe -- to the "uncivilized" regions of the world. He
leaves England feeling "something like an emissary of
light." But the Marlow who tells the tale is a changed
man. Early in the story he notes, "The conquest of the
earth, which mostly means the taking it away from those who
have a different complexion or slightly flatter noses than
ourselves, is not a pretty thing when you look into it too
much. What redeems it is the idea only." Once he arrives
at the Company's headquarters at the mouth of the Congo,
Marlow begins to be disillusioned by the greed, cruelty,
poverty, and violence which, if not exactly sanctioned by
"the idea," are at least its practical result. "The idea"
itself -- the moral value of civilization -- becomes the
central focus as Marlow continues his suspenseful journey
towards Kurtz. He admits his curiosity "to see whether
this man, who had come out equipped with moral ideas of
some sort, would climb to the top after all and how he
would set about his work when there."
    Conrad makes it clear that Kurtz is not simply an
idiosyncratic individual. He is emblematic of much of
European society and values: "All Europe contributed to
the making of Kurtz." Kurtz -- poet, painter, entrepreneur
-- is described as representing the best of western culture.
He is a "prodigy," a special being," a "universal genius."
Kurtz's fall is greater because his promise was so much

greater than the other Company men. The greed and insensitivity of the Company officials are logical extensions of an exploitive system. The manager is described as a "papier-mâché Mephistopheles." But Kurtz is something much different. He is, in language rich with ominous overtones, the "chief of the Inner States." Kurtz's exploration of the dark continent is but a metaphor for the exploration of the dark side of his own nature. Marlow believes Kurtz saw more of man's nature than would be possible within the confines of society. The result was that "his soul was mad. Being alone in the wilderness, it had looked within itself, and . . . it had gone mad." Freed from the artificial restraints of society, Kurtz was powerless to restrain himself: "The thing to know was what he belonged to, how many powers of darkness claimed him for their own." The most vivid and disturbing example of Kurtz's decline is represented by the heads on the stakes outside his house. As Marlow notes with characteristic English understatement: "They only showed that Mr. Kuurtz lacked restraint in the gratification of his various lusts, there was something wanting in him. . . ."

Despite Kurtz's abominable rites, Marlow is able to find some consolation in Kurtz's last words, "The horror! The horror!" They represent a moral victory to Marlow because they imply that Kurtz had not lost his moral bearings, that he had, after all, internalized some of the moral values of Western civilization. Some readers, however, may not be sure as Marlow. Conrad has shown how readily the restraints are abandoned. As Marlow notes when he begins to speak, it has only been a short time since England too "has been one of the dark places of the earth."

ARTHUR CONAN DOYLE

The Red-Headed League

(p. 320)

Some readers will consider Jabez Wilson, who opens the
story, too gullible to be credible. This might be so if he
played a more significant role in the story. As it is,
Wilson's purpose is little more than to introduce Holmes to
the mystery of the Red-Headed League and serve as a contrast
to Holmes's keen powers of observation and deduction. In
his tendency to allow his greed to get the better of his
common sense, Wilson may be more realistic than we care to
admit.

Only a few paragraphs into the tale, Holmes announces
that Dr. Watson "has been my partner and helper in many of
my most successful cases." The announcement informs us
that their relationship is more than a casual one. Indeed,
Holmes feels that Watson shares his "love of all that is
bizarre and outside the conventions" of daily life. Through
such statements, Doyle deftly binds Watson and Holmes with
common experiences and interests and strengthens the Doctor's
authority in the tale he is about to relate. We also learn
that Watson has chronicled previous Holmes adventures.
Thus, while lacking Holmes's ingenuity in solving mysteries,
Watson is an astute observer of Holmes, who might himself
be considered part of the bizarre and unconventional.

As in most of Doyle's stories, the mystery of the
moment is overshadowed by the mystery of Holmes himself.
That is to say, the emphasis is less on plot than on
character. The real interest of the tale comes from the
glimpses of Holmes's sharp powers of observation and
deduction, his usual mannerisms, his broad knowledge and

experience, and his "dual nature" -- "poetic and contemplative," as well as "relentless, keenwitted, [and] ready-handed."

Holmes's opening deductions about Mr. Wilson have nothing to do with the ensuing mystery, but do influence the way we respond to what follows. Holmes's observations, coming immediately after Watson's clear but unenlightening description of Wilson, establish respect for Holmes's techniques and powers of deduction. It forces us to take him seriously from that point on. It also alerts us to be on our guard for even the smallest clues.

A comparison of Holmes with Agatha Christie's famous detective, Hercule Poirot ("Double Sin," p. 500), shows several points of resemblance. Both are masters at connecting the seemingly unrelated pieces of a puzzle. Their success lies in their ability to look at each fact from more than one point of view, to weigh the significance of each event individually without sliding into any unwarranted assumptions. Like Poe's Dupin, Holmes and Poirot possess an artistic or creative as well as an analytical side. Each is seen through the limited perspective of the narrator-companion (as opposed to the omniscient point of view of the author) who stresses the detective's idiosyncracies as well as the mystery itself.

Unlike Poe in "The Purloined Letter," Doyle is less interested in theories of human nature than in creating a mystery around a vivid protagonist whose "brilliant reasoning power would rise to the level of intuition." His tale, while not profound, is interesting and entertaining. We are invited to match wits with Holmes, whose thoughts remain hidden while his actions are described carefully by Dr. Watson. Doyle keeps us in a state of suspense by continually showing us actions without giving us their cause or, in some cases, their result. (We do not know, for example, until the end of the tale the significance of the "white splash of acid" on Spaulding's face or the result of Holmes's vigorous thumping on the pavement.) Doyle leaves out just enough information to create suspense without losing our interest.

ANTON CHEKHOV

Gooseberries

Translated by Ivy Litvinov

(p. 335)

The gooseberries symbolize very different things to the two
brothers. For Nikolai they come to represent his long
sought dream of becoming a part of the landed gentry.
There is a hint early in the story that his affection for
estate life is linked to the carefree days of youth when
both boys "roamed the fields" and experienced the "freedom of
the countryside." The irony for Nikolai is that his dreams of
success and freedom have come to enslave him. He becomes
discontented, stingy, and, finally, married to a woman he
does not love. Most of his life is over before he begins
life as a country gentleman; when he finally does so, it is
not the beauty and freedom of the country that he enjoys but
rather his sense of superiority over the peasants. In his
new life as one of the landed gentry Nikolai becomes "stout
and flabby." His insensitivity is shown in his shallow
maxims, his superficial interest in religion and good
works, and his treatment of the peasants.

   The culmination of Nikolai's quest for the good life
comes when he tastes the first fruits of his gooseberry
bushes. The fact that they are sour and unripe does not
affect his enjoyment. He has long since defined happiness
as the ability to grow them; he has invested too much of
himself in his quest to doubt that the gooseberries are
anything but "delicious." Ivan quotes Pushkin's line that
"the lie which elates us is dearer than a thousand sober
truths" to suggest how out of touch with reality his brother
has become. Nikolai has no use for sober truth. His
illusions leave him more inebriated than his drunken
peasants.

Ivan is right when he states that the story is about himself, not Nikolai. He realizes that he has shared many of his brother's values and attitudes towards the peasantry. Observing his brother's "happiness" forces Ivan to reevaluate his own beliefs. He realizes that a nostalgic escape from city life is "a sort of renunciation . . . without faith." Even the noblest dreams, theories, or ideas can lull us into passivity and unawareness. A distant goal of happiness is false if it forces us to deny the present. Reality, even if "hard and sour," is better than an illusion.

ANTON CHEKHOV ≡≡≡≡

The Kiss

Translated by Robert N. Linscott

(p. 342)

Chekov begins the tale of Riabovich's memorable experience
with realistic details and description. We are told the
exact time and date when the N Artillery Brigade arrives at
the village of Miestechky. We hear the invitation for tea
at General von Rabbek's and watch the nineteen officers
reluctantly prepare to attend, dreading that they may be
subjected to listening to the retired general's past
adventures. Long before we first see Staff-Captain Riabovich
we are given a minute description of the host and hostess
and the casual nature of the gathering. Chekhov's vivid
description of the young ladies, the rich spring odors of
poplar leaves, roses, and lilacs, the music and dancing, all
set the stage for an adventurous evening. By slow degrees
our attention becomes focused on the short, round-shouldered,
undistinguished Riabovich, who feels the valse and the
cognac "mingling tipsily." The significance of the kiss is
not simply that it happened but that it happened to him,
one who had long since "grown reconciled to his own
insignificance."

In contrast to the "profoundly dull" routine of his
artillery service, the kiss appears a "mysterious, romantic
adventure" to the young Captain. He forgets his shyness
and his self-doubts and begins to enjoy the evening. He
realizes that the mystery is easily explained, that "the
mistake was likely enough," and spends the rest of the
evening trying to guess the identity of his unknown
benefactor. It is significant that he settles on none of
them but instead composes a portrait of their various
charms. He leaves with a "clear vision" of a girl who is

45

"nowhere to be seen."

In the ensuing months, despite his attempts to reason that the kiss had no significance, Riabovich's imagination begins to re-create and intensify his experience. Even the routine of military life cannot break the magic spell; the vision of the imaginary girl who kissed him "never afterwards forsook him." So powerful is Riabovich's imagination that he begins to act like a man in love. He is amazed that when he attempts to tell his adventure to his companions it only takes a minute. All he can tell are the facts, not their emotional significance.

Students may debate the meaning of the last paragraphs. Certainly the magic spell is broken and Riabovich once more sees his life as "thin and colorless." On the other hand, by choosing not to accept the general's second invitation the captain may be choosing to hold on to at least a little of something "uncommonly good and radiant" which had come into his life.

O. HENRY
(WILLIAM SYDNEY PORTER)

The Cop and the Anthem

(p. 353)

The most noticeable quality of this story is the extreme
contrast between Soapy's low economic and social status and
the elaborate vocabulary and sophisticated syntax in which
his adventures are related. (Students should be encouraged
to look up the meaning of such words as "soporific," "Boreas,"
"hegira," and "eleemosynary" and discuss their effect on the
story.) Not until several paragraphs into the tale do we
even realize that Soapy is a New York bum. He is given
none of the traditional tags which usually describe a
fictional character. "Soapy" is obviously a nickname. O.
Henry creates interest and a little suspense by leaving out
Soapy's origins, past misfortunes, and even his name. He
might be just another vagrant in a big city. The allusions,
the educated tone of the language, however, suggest that
Soapy is far from typical. The third paragraph begins,
"Soapy's mind became cognizant of the fact that the time
had come for him to resolve himself into a singular Committee
of Ways and Means to provide against the coming rigor."
Either the author is having fun at the expense of the city's
unfortunates, or Soapy is not a typical New York hobo.

Further events suggest the latter. We see that Soapy
not only has good taste (a roasted mallard duck, Chablis,
Camembert, and a dollar cigar!) but also a sense of personal
dignity. He realizes that in some ways "the Law was more
benign than Philanthropy"; that one must "pay in humiliation
of spirit" for every loaf of bread received from charity.
He feels that he would rather be a "guest of law" than
suffer the "personal inquisition" of philanthropic
organizations. Through Soapy's reflections and his futile

attempts to get arrested, O. Henry makes several acute observations on human nature, and on life in a densely populated yet strongly impersonal city.

The last paragraphs mark a dramatic shift in tone and imagery. Elaborate circumlocutions are replaced by simple, homely images which reveal a different side of our hero. The organ music stirs "immaculate thoughts," recalls earlier, more promising days, and awakens Soapy's desire to "make a man of himself again." The ironic reversal of the climax appropriately reenforces the view of the cold, impersonal nature of the city that we've seen throughout and gives us some insight into Soapy's earlier attitude and behavior.

MIGUEL DE UNAMUNO

Juan Manso:
A Dead Man's Tale

(p. 358)

Spanish born Unamuno was a poet, novelist, and playwright as
well as a short story writer. He lived during a time (1864-
1930) when traditional values and religious orthodoxy were
being replaced by modern skepticism and an existential view
of the world as a somewhat absurd place. The tale of Juan
Manso reflects aspects of both the traditional and modern
views of man and God.

    The images used to portray life after death are both
amusing and disconcertingly familiar. Like illegal aliens,
the departed souls mill around a registration room, and
push and shove their way past "a kind of immigration
control." Unamuno compares the scene to that outside the
ticket booth on the day of a big bullfight. The angels
resemble policemen keeping order. The people curse, entreat,
and insult each other as they scramble to learn their fate.
Even the "humble" friar is a con artist, "advancing pathetic
arguments" in order to advance himself. We see that in
heaven as on earth people and things are not always what
they appear to be.

    Juan continues his meek ways in heaven and soon becomes
a victim of his own reputation. He appears powerless to
assert himself. The Lord's surprising comment, "let him
look out for himself," suggests that Juan's meekness may not
necessarily be a virtue. Upon taking a closer look at
Juan's actions and attitudes we see that he is not so much
kind-hearted as he is passive and apathetic. He speaks
well of everyone, although he has "a bad opinion of
everybody," because he does not want to upset the even
tenor of his days. His favorite maxim, "never commit yourself,

and stick to the person who can help you the most," reflects
a passive selfishness. It explains his behavior both on
earth and in heaven. Juan never commits or acts; dying,
the author tells us, was "the only definite thing he ever
did in his life." Just as his meekness was "no avail
against the finality of death," neither does it serve to
get him within the walls of paradise. Juan expects a reward
although he did not risk anything for it. The secondary
definition of meek -- "deficient in spirit and courage" --
applies to Juan as readily as does the concept of humility.
Through the Lord's last words to Juan, the author implies
that the meek belong in heaven provided they are not
escapists who purchase their tranquility at the price of
all else.

SAKI
(H. H. MUNRO)

The Open Window

(p. 362)

In comparing "The Open Window" with "Double Sin," "The Red-Headed League," or "The Purloined Letter," students may note the difference between surprise and suspense. Saki gives us no eccentric or memorable detective pondering evidence which we too can see but not understand. We might easily overlook what "clues" are given because we are not told that a mystery is at hand. The tale seems to be over as soon as it has begun. The penultimate paragraph quickly alters our impression of the niece and, consequently, of all of the preceding events.

Upon rereading this brief tale we find that Saki has been very carefully manipulating our responses from the opening sentence. Now the clues appear to be everywhere, but carefully camouflaged by other details and impressions. For example, the author warns us that the niece is a "very self-possessed young lady" three times; he balances this, however, by also referring to her three times as "the child." We are quickly put off the scent in the second paragraph when we are given the impression -- or perhaps we just assume -- that the story is to be about Nuttel. His peculiar name, his uneasiness, his doubts, and his "nerve cure" all serve to focus our attention on him and his reactions to the story he hears and the subsequent events. We are told of Nuttel's private doubts in the second paragraph, yet are never told what's going on in the child's mind.

Saki's experience as a journalist and writer of short humorous essays holds him in good stead in this story's quick pace, short paragraphs, life-like conversation, and vivid description. Romance -- that is, an elaborate or embellished account or explanation -- "at short notice" is not only the niece's speciality, but Saki's as well.

STEPHEN CRANE

The Open Boat

(p. 365)

The opening sentence grabs the attention of most readers because it immediately restricts them to the point of view of the four men in the boat. We seem not to be reading of an adventure long after the fact but to be on hand as it unfolds. Crane conveys a sense of immediacy, of danger, in the first sentence by dispensing with any introduction and beginning with a description of the world as seen from this small boat being tossed about on the waves. None knew the color of the sky because their gaze was riveted upon the next oncoming wave: ". . . all of the men knew the colors of the sea." Crane continues this perspective in paragraph eleven in which he writes that the "process of the breaking day was unknown to them. They were aware only of this effect upon the color of the waves that rolled toward them." The graphic description of dawn which begins section 7 is conveyed in the same manner.

By limiting the perspective to that of the four men, Crane vividly conveys the hopes, doubts, fears, and the physical and mental exhaustion of the boatmen. We see them go from smoking cigars "with an assurance of an impending rescue shining in their eyes" to thoughts of impending death in an indifferent universe. As their states of mind and body change during their struggle, so does the tone of the narrative. The tone and diction change from mildly ironic to serious to despairing to absurdly formal to realistic. The men in the boat may represent a microcosm in the sense that all of us experience the widely changing moods and emotions of the four men, although not in such a short time or in such unusual conditions.

The struggle against the overwhelming forces of nature
does create a "subtle brotherhood" among the men. The
correspondent realizes that it "was the best experience of
his life." But he also realizes man's insignificant place
in the universe. He comes to his first realization that
nature is not even against him; she is "indifferent, flatly
indifferent." The shipwreck, for example, is not a malicious
act of an evil force, it is simply "apropos of nothing."
The correspondent's awareness of what is termed the "unconcern
of the universe" is very similar to Crane's poem "A Man
Said to the Universe," published two years after "The Open
Boat":

> A man said to the universe:
> "Sir, I exist!"
> "However," replied the universe,
> "The fact has not created in me
> A sense of obligation."

The correspondent's first response to his situation is
anger. But he soon realizes that "there are no bricks and
no temples," there is only the ongoing process of nature.
Portrayed as both beautiful and dangerous, nature's dominant
characteristic is its indifference to human concerns. "A
high cold star on a winter's night" is as close as it comes
to answering our questions concerning the meaning of life
and death. The death of the oiler, probably the most
capable of all four men, dramatically confirms the
correspondent's new awareness of an indifferent universe.

Paul's Case

(p. 381)

The word "case" has a formal, objective connotation not
found in a word like "story" or "situation." In a legal
case or a mystery case there is usually an expectation that
certain facts or motives can be uncovered. As we read of
Paul's case we are faced with a complex human being who
doesn't himself understand many of the reasons for his
actions; nevertheless, we attempt to make sense of the
events, to discover a cause which will explain the effect,
to find a motive. We seek to understand Paul's actions and
feelings and our own response to them.

Most people in Paul's world do not seek to understand
him on any significant emotional level. To the faculty of
Pittsburgh High School Paul is simply another case, another
example of unruly conduct and "impertinence." Neither does
Paul's father make any attempt to understand that his son
may have different dreams and values than many young men on
Cordelia Street. Cather's description of the young clerk
held up as a model for Paul suggests that he may be near-
sighted in more ways than one. Students may be divided
about whether or not society has caused Paul's problems.
In any case, society offers little sympathy or incentive to
a young man who values his imaginative world of romance, of
"cool things and soft lights and fresh flowers," over what
Cather terms "the flavourless, colourless mass of every-day
existence."

Cather repeatedly emphasizes Paul's desire for escape
through her description of his passionate response to music,
art, and theater. Through the arts Paul is able to free
himself from the dullness of daily life, to enter into a
world of fantasy and beauty. It is at the theater, we are

told, that Paul "really lived." Like the wings of Icarus,
Paul's fascination with beauty is both the means of his escape
and the source of his destruction. He commits his crime in
order to momentarily be a part of the world of elegance and
beauty. Everywhere he looks he sees the "glaring affirmation
of the omnipotence of wealth," and comes to believe that
money is the only means by which he can experience the life
he has dreamed of. His desire for escape from his assigned
role in "the immense design of things" is stronger than
reason or even caution. Not until he has thrown himself
at the train does "the folly of his haste" even occur to him.

THOMAS MANN

Disorder and Early Sorrow

Translated by H. T. Lowe-Porter

(p. 394)

The setting of postwar Germany plays a major part in this
story. The "desolate and distracted times" following the
loss of World War I are a period of unbridled inflation and
uncertain social distinctions and expectations. Mann
examines how the different characters adjust to the
unprecedented times. The ladies Hinterhofer are painfully
aware of their fall from the middle class to the role of
servants. Xaver, "having been born to low life instead of
achieving it," has a much easier time. He has an air of
independence and gusto lacking in the other servants. The
big folk, having known no other life, accept the postwar
conditions much more easily than their parents. They make a
sport out of their weekly quest to wring twenty eggs out of
the shopkeeper, and are more comfortable with their modest
means and simple clothing. The middle-class parents,
however, find things rather difficult. The Professor is
disturbed that at times he cannot tell his son from his
servant. He "displays a middle-class ambitiousness" and
clings to the manners and affectations of that station.

    The Professor takes refuge from the disorder of society
in his historical studies and in his love for his little
daughter. For the Professor the two are intricately related.
He ponders the relationship between the two early in the
story when he muses on the historian's love for the "coherent,
disciplined, historic past . . . the temper of eternity"
which assuages the "excesses of the present." He also
reflects that "his sense of the eternal . . . has found in
his love for his little daughter a way to save itself from
the wounding inflicted by the times." For all his claims

of scientific objectivity the Professor never quite sees or
fully accepts the nature of his love for Ellie. He admits
"in the interest of science" that there is "something not
perfectly right and good in his love" but goes no further.
He refuses to see her as a little person who will grow and
change in unexpected ways. She is a symbol of something
beautiful, graceful, and timeless. Similarly, the Professor's
historical studies, appropriately enough on the Counter-
Reformation, do not help him understand or accept the
present but serve to insulate him from his own time. Only
superficially does he understand that for a historian such
as himself the past is honored because it is dead, that
"death is the root of all . . . abiding significance."

The Professor's love for his daughter and for history
is life-denying. It binds him to a conservative ideal
which keeps him from being a creative part of the ever-
changing present. His unease is reflected in his emphasis
upon correct manners and proper phrases -- (his mot juste,
for example, strikes him as "a very bulwark") -- as well as
his outrage over his little girl's infatuation with Herr
Hergesell. Although the Professor's tenderness for her is
quite real, the episode holds no insight for him. The last
sentence shows him finding solace by putting off the
inevitable and desperately clinging to past events and a
relationship which his daughter will soon outgrow.

SHERWOOD ANDERSON

I'm a Fool

(p. 415)

"I'm a Fool" is one of Anderson's many portraits of small
town American life. The character of the swipe is
representative of the attitudes of many who share his
economic and cultural background. Through the skillful use
of slang and point of view, Anderson allows the swipe to
reveal his passions and prejudices much more effectively
than if the story were simply told about him. Although
much of the slang is outdated, it is effective because it
accurately reflects the swipe's personality, age, and social
position. Despite his own declaration to the contrary, the
swipe's language gives him away as being uneducated and
provincial. Yet it also reflects his youthful energy and
enthusiasm.

The Adventures of Huckleberry Finn is the prototype
for such stories as this in which the slang and the first-
person narration allow us to see qualities and contradictions
which the youthful narrator isn't aware of. The swipe
possesses several of Huck's characteristics as well. Huck
would have agreed with the swipe's remark that "boys who
are raised regular in houses, and never have a fine nigger
like Burt for best friend, and go to high schools and
college, and never steal anything, or get drunk a little,
or learn to swear from fellows who know how . . . don't
know nothing at all. They've never had no opportunity."

But the swipe is not as comfortable with this view of
life as he would have us believe. He is too insecure to be
at ease either as a swipe or a spectator in the best seat
in the grandstand. Paragraph 10, for example, shows the
swipe's sensitivity to nature and enthusiasm for his simple

lifestyle but ends abruptly with the defensive comment:
"You can stick your colleges up your nose for all of me."
His repeated insistence that his lifestyle is superior to
all others only underscores his sense of inferiority and
envy. His rude manner toward the man with the cane and
Windsor tie reflects the swipe's insecurity. He has "another
drink of whiskey, just to show him something."

Anderson prepares us for the events at the track by
setting them within the framework of the narrator's experience
as a swipe during the past year. Although he doesn't
realize it, the swipe's account of his adventures shows
that he is neither responsible nor truthful. He has no
qualms about going through Mr. Mathers's house uninvited,
opening his wine, or driving his prize horse. When asked
questions about racing, "all you did was to lie and lie all
you could." Although the swipe realizes he has made a big
mistake lying to the "peachy" girl at the track, he doesn't
see it as being consistent with his character and lifestyle
of the past year. He still blames much of his mistake on
the whiskey and the man in the Windsor tie. His moral
perspective is best summed up in his own words: "I've
always thought to myself, 'put up a good front' and so I
did it."

JAMES JOYCE

The Dead

(p. 423)

"The Dead" is an appropriate conclusion to Dubliners, a
collection of stories in which James sought to reflect the
moral paralysis of his native country. As in several of
the stories, Joyce gives us a richly textured account of
the Irish middle class. Characters such as Gabriel, the
Misses Morgan, and Mr. Browne are not unusual in Irish
fiction. It is Joyce's vivid portrait of them which creates
a memorable account of a rather ordinary and, in many ways,
very dull Christmas party. Joyce is able to give us a
sense of the idiosyncrasies of Freddy, Mr. Browne, Gabriel,
and the others while simultaneously conveying a sense that
the hostesses and their guests are not having a party so
much as going through their assigned roles.
     Mary Jane, for example, plays her customary piece and
all applaud, the loudest applause coming from the young men
in the doorway who have not even listened. Gabriel, of
course, is the most obvious one who does not allow himself
any spontaneous response to the people and events around
him. His preoccupation with his after-dinner speech reflects
his insecurity. He takes refuge in polite, correct, formal
behavior and conversation. His interactions with Lily and
Miss Ivors leave him disconcerted. Lily's remarks leave
Gabriel "discomposed" and Miss Ivors's teasing throws him
off balance for the rest of the evening. He has no polite
or ready-made answers for their sharp remarks. At the end
of the story, however, Gabriel experiences what Joyce terms
an "epiphany," in which he is able to step out of his usual
roles and see the true nature of things. After talking
with his wife of Michael Furey, Gabriel has an insight into

the nature of his past behavior. He is overcome with a
"shameful consciousness" of his own person. "He saw himself
as a ludicrous figure, acting as a penny boy for his aunts,
a nervous, well-meaning sentimentalist, orating to vulgarians
and idealizing his own clownish lusts." Gabriel comes to
realize that Michael Furey is more alive in Gretta's heart
than are most of those at the party. He realizes too that
it is better to live and die "in the full glory of some
passion, than fade and wither dismally with age."

Joyce has prepared us for this realization throughout
the story. The ironic contrasts between the forced gaiety
of the party on Usher's Island and its underlying lifelessness,
between the old single-minded spinsters and the painting of
Romeo and Juliet, cause us to wonder if the title of the
story does not apply to those who are physically alive but
spirtually empty. In the midst of the party Gabriel longs
to escape into the cool oblivion of the snow; at the end
the snow has become richly symbolic. Gabriel's realization
that death, like the snow, is "general all over Ireland,"
his acceptance of death and simultaneously of the true
nature of his past life make him an appropriate vehicle for
Joyce's vision. Like the archangel of the Bible, this
Gabriel, in the end, becomes a messenger of truth and
insight.

JAMES JOYCE

Araby

(p. 450)

The theme of "Araby," as of many of the stories in <u>Dubliners</u>, is disillusionment and disenchantment. In this case a boy discovers the gap that exists between magical words, mental images, hopes, and the dull reality of things in a city "hostile to romance." The glamorously archaic word "Araby," with its "Eastern enchantment" and exotic connotations, refers, as it turns out, to a prosaic church bazaar. The sensitive boy's first experience of love is presented through finely perceived details and the luxuriant imagery of religion and courtly love. His "confused adoration" is a "chalice" born by an acolyte "through a throng of foes"; the girl's name appears in "strange prayers and praises"; he experiences ecstasy at the very sound of the words "love" and "Araby." His mission to buy something for his true love at the fair perhaps lacks the heroism of a knight's errand, but its poetic connection with many romantic folk-ballads is evident.

The narrator, however, does not view his younger self with much sympathy. He speaks of his "foolish blood," of "innumerable follies" that "laid waste [his] waking and sleeping thoughts," and adds no comment to soften the moment of disillusion expressed in the final sentence: "Gazing up into the darkness I saw myself as a creature driven and derided by vanity; and my eyes burned with anguish and anger." Even though boys can be temporarily "set free" from school and play till their bodies glow amid the "brown imperturbable faces" of North Richmond Street, boyhood offers no real -- and not even a nostalgic -- escape from the paralysis of the Dubliners' "decent lives." The fact that Mangan's sister, the object of the boy's love, is described as a "brown figure" and is most often seen when she calls her brother for his routine tea, predicts the inevitability of romantic disillusionment.

The term "epiphany" that Joyce applied to the moments of insight in these sketches is doubly ironic in "Araby," if one compares the loss of hope experienced by the boy to the mystical manifestation witnessed by the Magi, and realizes that the boy's revelation occurs, symbolically, at the moment when the lights go out.

Ivy Day in the Committee Room

(p. 455)

Joyce once described his volume of short stories, <u>Dubliners</u>, as follows: "My intention was to write a chapter of the moral history of my country and I chose Dublin for the scene because that city seemed to me the centre of the paralysis. I have tried to present it . . . under four of its aspects: childhood, adolescence, maturity, and public life." "Ivy Day in the Committee Room" clearly fits into the final category and was, interestingly, Joyce's own favorite among his stories. The reason for this positive assessment of a story that might seem particularly dry to younger readers is probably the perfect interconnection of theme and technique that it presents. The very lack of interesting events, the trivial dialogue and the flat realism of description, express the paralysis and moral emptiness of the lives of the Dubliners. Unlike earlier short story writers, Joyce refuses to use artificial contrivances to make his plot superficially interesting.

The mundane scene in the committee room, presented in what Joyce called "a style of scrupulous meanness," takes place on Ivy Day -- the anniversary of Irish politician Charles Stewart Parnell's death. The latter's forceful leadership in the fight for Irish self-government and his attractiveness as a personality are implicitly brought into contrast with the petty canvassers and their candidate. Joyce describes these men with fastidious detachment: old Jack with his moist, mechanically munching mouth, the gray-haired and pimply O'Connor, the snuffling and spitting Henchy, the oxlike Crofton. The fact that they are soliciting votes for a man they cannot even trust to pay their own wages reflects their lack of political idealism. The ivy

leaves they sport and their occasional nostalgic, or merely
perfunctory, references to Parnell are thus meaningless.
Only Joe Hynes shows some evidence of loyalty to the cause
of Irish nationalism and the rights of the working man, but
he is regarded with suspicion by his colleague Henchy.

The "epiphany" of this sketch, the moment of intensified
insight into the lives of these men, is provided by Hynes's
reciting of his poem on the death of Parnell. It is,
however, a deeply ironic epiphany, as it sharply reveals to
the readers the men's lack of insight into their own moral
position. The poem is dubbed "a very fine piece of writing,"
but its political meaning is ignored.

VIRGINIA WOOLF ===

Kew Gardens

(p. 466)

"Kew Gardens" is an effective piece despite the fact -- or,
perhaps, because of the fact -- that it avoids many of the
traditional techiques of the short story form. It has
little plot or conflict in the conventional sense. Some
students may question whether "Kew Gardens" should be termed
a short story. Those who enjoy it will be those who can
enjoy its vivid imagery and fragmentary glimpses of life in
the gardens without insisting on a traditional plot or on
character development.
        The point of view, also, is unusual. As in an omniscient
narrative, we are told the thoughts and feelings of several
characters, yet none is explored in any detail. We get
only a brief glance before encountering the musings and
memories of another pair strolling past the snail. Our
sense of the fragmented, subjective nature of reality is
heightened by the personification of the snail, who has his
own unique perspective on life in Kew Gardens. Point of
view is not used to unify the various diverse elements or
explain them, but simply to present senses of reality which
together make up the reality of the garden. Although at
first the various couples appear distinct and clearly
distinguishable, we soon sense that each particular element,
each plant, animal, or person, is a part of something larger
which functions "like a vast nest of Chinese boxes all of
wrought steel turning ceaselessly one within another."
        Woolf achieves a sense of unity overarching the diverse
realities within the garden through imagery which ties them
all together. Not only is the snail personified but all of
nature appears sentient. The leaves are "heart-shaped" and

67

"tongue shaped" and the flowers flash their gorgeous colors into the air. Nature and human nature are carefully blended. The movements of the men and women walking past the flowers resemble the zig-zag flights of the white and blue butterflies. Similarly Simon's memories of his early love, appropriately named Lily, center not on words but images, a silver buckle and a dragon fly. The musings of the elderly man combine natural images -- such as the forests of Uruguay with their tropical roses, nightingales, and beaches -- with those of fantasy, such as mermaids and spirits. The most exquisite blending of the different realities of the garden is captured in Woolf's description of the ponderous woman who "looked through the pattern of falling words at the flowers standing cool, firm, and upright in the earth. . . . She stood there letting the words fall over her, swaying the top part of her body slowly backwards and forwards, looking at the flowers."

FRANZ KAFKA

A Hunger Artist

Translated by Willa and Edwin Muir

(p. 471)

Students may vary widely in their attitudes toward the
hunger artist. Some may see him as self-centered or
ensnared in self-destructive dreams of fame and fortune.
Others may find his honesty and dedication to his art
admirable. Kafka veils his own attitude through a tone and
a point of view both objective and confidential. He describes
the world of the hunger artist -- the various types of
spectators, the relays of permanent watchers, the impresario,
and the circus crowds -- but also conveys some sense of the
feelings and opinions of the hunger artist toward his art
and his patrons.

The term "hunger artist" itself invites ambivalent
responses. We usually think of an artist as one who creates,
not simply abstains or goes without. On the other hand,
the hunger artist resembles other artists in his separation
from normal human activity and his need to practice his art:
"'. . . I have to fast, I can't help it,' said the hunger
artist." In his inability to enjoy common food, to be
nourished by that which most people accept, the hunger
artist represents many artists who cannot accept the habits,
lifestyles, or morals of their contemporaries. The cage of
the hunger artist is a symbol of both his separation from
society and his freedom. Within it he is free to practice
his art and study those who come to watch.

Kafka underscores the artist's need for some contact
with society through the hunger artist's relationship with
the impresario and his feelings toward his fame and eventual
decline. Although he feels that he is being cheated of the
fame he deserves as "the record hunger artist of all time,"

he nevertheless submits to the impresario's dictate that
forty days is the limit to any fast. The impresario is the
hunger artist's connecting link to the everyday world of
commerce and self-interest. It is he who astutely realizes
that after forty days local interest and sympathetic support
began to decline -- despite "a steadily increasing pressure
of advertisement." The hunger artist longs to endure a
fast "beyond human imagination." The impresario, however,
knows -- and the hunger artist eventually discovers -- that
beyond human imagination is also beyond human sympathy. It
doesn't pay.

The hunger artist disdains many of his watchers and
feels himself fighting against "a whole world of
nonunderstanding." Yet without some interest from the
outside world, the hunger artist discovers that he has lost
track of time and the length of his record-breaking fast.
When he first joined the circus he had hoped to "astound
the world" by his unprecedented performance. Later he
feels cheated by the neglect he suffers. His loss of social-
and self-respect is reflected in his new location near the
menagerie. The crowd, no longer moved by the art of fasting,
streams past the hunger artist to observe a new phenomenon.
They ignore the life-consuming dedication of the hunger
artist and instead flock to observe the young panther in
which "the joy of life streamed with such ardent passion."

D. H. LAWRENCE

The Horse Dealer's Daughter

(p. 477)

"He had no intention of loving her: his whole will was against his yielding. It was horrible. And yet wonderful was the touch of her shoulders, beautiful the shining of her face . . . He had a horror of yielding to her. Yet something in him ached also." These sentences reflect Lawrence's central concern of the powerful struggle within every individual between the will and the passions, between the conscious, rational faculties and the less explicable but perhaps more compelling urges of body and spirit. Fergusson falls in love with Mabel against his will. His common sense as well as sense of "professional honour" tell him that his experience is crazy. "He had never wanted to love her . . . he had no single personal thought of her." But the powerful subliminal forces, the sexual and spiritual longings, awakened by the rescue and its aftermath transcend personal considerations. The experience has stripped both the doctor and Mabel of their old identities and left them vulnerable to more profound, elemental life forces. Without warning, both find themselves in a highly charged emotional, physical, and spiritual state which they neither understand nor desire.

Lawrence begins the story in a conventional, realistic manner. We are introduced to the Pervin family at a crucial point in the lives of each member. We are told how the three brothers will respond to the dissolution of the family business. Mabel, "impassive and inscrutable," remains something of a mystery in this first part. Once the point of view switches to Mabel, we begin to understand her love for her mother, her "animal pride," and calm acceptance of

death. "For the life she followed here in the world was
far less real than the world of death she inherited from
her mother." In his description of Mabel, Lawrence alters
his realism in favor of a poetic account of her feelings
and her mesmerizing effect on the doctor as he passes the
graveyard. The description of the rescue in the "foul
earthy water" is both very graphic and highly symbolic.
Lawrence employs the baptism/re-birth imagery to convey the
profound significance of the experience. (The story was
originally called "Miracle"). They are reborn from their
finite, earthy, individual selves into contact with something
mysterious, transcendent, and compelling. The doctor finds
that Mabel holds "the life of his body in her hands and
that he is powerless to free himself." Lawrence's movement
from the realistic to the richly symbolic reflects Mabel's
and Ferguson's -- and the reader's -- shift to a concern
for the spiritual and sexual passions which lie beneath our
preoccupation for proper social behavior.

D. H. LAWRENCE

The Rocking-Horse Winner

(p. 489)

"The Rocking-Horse Winner" is Lawrence's fable on the high price of success in our materialistic, consumption-oriented society. He is skeptical of a society or a value system which prizes money over the less tangible but more vital qualities such as love or a sense of family or community. Lawrence sees the modern world, with its strong emphasis on material gain, as a threat to man's spirtual nature. It suppresses his better qualities and harnesses his energies into the service of what Nick Carroway in The Great Gatsby terms "a vast, vulgar, meritricious beauty."

Paul's parents are a part of this modern world with its slick commercial beauty and emphasis on success. Despite the shortage of money they "lived in style." The father indulges his expensive tastes and the mother gives the impression of being a concerned parent. Their social position is maintained although their marriage is a failure, their "love turned to dust." Anxiety over money is omnipresent. The wife bitterly blames the husband for their lack of success. The children feel the tension and see its effect on their mother. Although all of them hear the incessant whisper in the house, "There must be more money! There must be more money!," none speaks of it. The fear it inspires cannot be rationally understood or explained by the children. It can only be communicated non-verbally: "They would look into each other's eyes, to see if they had all heard. And each one saw in the eyes of the other two that they had heard."

In his attempt to ease his mother's financial worries, to soften her hard heart, and stop the whispering, Paul

becomes a victim of a commercially-oriented society.
Despite his success with the horses and his five-thousand
pound present to his mother, life does not become easier
for Paul or his family. Material success does not result
in happiness as Paul had hoped. As she read the letter
telling of the unexpected money, Hester's "face hardened
and became more expressionless." Material prosperity
cannot satisfy our emotional or spiritual needs and often
results in increasing our dependence on material comforts.
Paul finds that although their lifestyle is better than
before, the voices did not cease but instead "simply trilled
and screamed in a sort of ecstasy: 'There must be more
money!'" Frightened at this unexpected result, Paul becomes
"wild-eyed and strange."

The vivid descriptions of Paul's eyes are one means by
which Lawrence conveys Paul's metamorphosis from naive
child to passionate victim of the modern worship of success.
In his early conversation with his mother about the nature
of luck and money, Paul watches her "with unsure eyes."
Later they are described as a "blue glare," "flaring," "big
hot blue eyes," "blue fire," "cold fire," "blazing" and
finally like a "blue stone." By the end of the story Paul
has outgrown the nursery. He not only eats with his parents
but has adopted their financial worries and preoccupations.
He feels the social pressure of their lack of money: the
whispers are "like people laughing at you behind your back."
Paul doesn't realize that money can't stop the whispering
nor can it create warmth or affection where there isn't
any. Lawrence shows us the irony of equating luck (i.e.,
good fortune) with money. Indeed "filthy lucre" and "filthy
lucker" become synonomous, as Paul had originally -- and
quite innocently -- believed. His innocence is only the
first installment paid toward the high price of success.
Ultimately it costs him his life.

AGATHA CHRISTIE

Double Sin

(p. 500)

Like Sherlock Holmes and Dr. Watson, Poirot and Hastings
are revealed to the reader largely through contrast.
Hastings serves as a foil to offset Poirot's less adventurous,
but more thorough, approach to both motor coaches and mysteries.

By making Hastings both narrator and actor, Christie
allows us to participate in the action. Events are revealed
to us precisely as they are to the narrator and to Poirot.
Such a point of view adds to the suspense of the story
because it allows us to see the events and, at the same
time, forces us to speculate as to their significance. Had
the story been told from Poirot's point of view or from
that of an omniscient narrator, the reader would not have had
to participate; thus the element of suspense would have
been lost. The disadvantage of such an approach is that
our perceptions are limited to those of the narrator. If
we are given a strong sense of the narrator's emotional and
moral perspective, we can make allowances for whatever
shortcomings or biases we may perceive.

Hastings is not dull-witted; he is, however, as his
name implies, hasty in his judgments and conclusions. He
returns "full of enthusiasm" for the motor coach excursion
even though he has only "inquired a few particulars." In
his desire to aid the pretty young lady and solve the
mystery, Hastings makes several understandable but unfounded
assumptions which lead to erroneous conclusions.

Early in the story Poirot is portrayed as a rather
unusual combination of qualities: he is careful, even over-
cautious, restrained, curious, parsimonious, and meticulous.
These qualities cause him to pay close attention to the

75

details of the train schedule, haggle over the ticket price, pay close attention to the young man who books passage only as far as Monkhampton, and notice the young lady's interest in the young man, all of which would prove to be important factors later in the story. Poirot's own habit of cultivating the "art" of the moustache causes him to notice the young man "trying to grow" one. Similarly, his restraint keeps him several times from responding to the laughs and winning ways of the young lady on the motor coach.

In comparing Poirot with Sherlock Holmes, we see that the methods of the two detectives are clear reflections of their characters. Poirot is described as "a strange mixture of Flemish thrift and artistic fervour," a mixture which makes him both cautious and creative. The first paragraph lets us know that Poirot, like Holmes, relies on his instincts as well as his perceptions and his reasoning powers. (See also the comments on "The Red-Headed League.")

KATHERINE ANNE PORTER ≡≡≡

Flowering Judas

(p. 510)

Because this tale is set in Mexico during a period of widespread
social unrest and revolutionary activity, it may be useful
to recall that Porter herself was involved in the Obregon
Revolution after she moved to Mexico in 1921. Revolutionaries
are often considered traitors and the title itself recalls
one of history's most infamous traitors. But Porter is
less concerned with movements than with individuals.
"Flowering Judas" is a study in character. Braggioni is a
memorable example of one type of traitor. Although he is
praised by his followers for possessing "a love of humanity
raised above mere personal affections," we can see that power
is his real love. He takes pains to be a "good revolutionist
and professional lover of humanity" because it affords him
the lifestyle and influence he craves. As the author
states, "he will never die of it." He has changed a great
deal from the young poet and dreamer he once was. The
revolution which was once a dream to him is now viewed as
simply another business. He despises those he manipulates
and has traded his ideal for thirty pieces of silver -- a
scented silk handkerchief and rich food.
     Laura is attempting to keep herself free from such
worldly temptation. She views Braggioni as "a symbol of
her many disillusions." Although she is unable to define
precisely the nature of her devotion, motives, or obligations,
she knows that she draws her strength to carry on from her
ability to resist the lure of worldly pleasures. Her refusal
to wear lace reflects her commitment to her cause; instead,
she wears "the uniform of an idea." Porter does not tell
us the history or value of the cause. What is significant

is that Laura approaches her political activity with a
religious fervor. Her Catholic upbringing holds her in
good stead in her quest to become "a vessel of abstract
virtue," her ideal of a true revolutionary: "She has
encased herself in a set of principles derived from her
early training." Even now she risks scandal by slipping
off to church to say a Hail Mary. (Interestingly, the word
"laura" is defined as "a monastery of an Eastern Church".)

Despite her devotion and hard work among the school
children and the prisoners, Laura is often torn between her
ideals and her sense of the realities of the situation.
Even her comrades suggest she is a hopeless romantic for
holding to her abstract ideal of what a revolution and a
revolutionary should be. Yet Laura is not comfortable
with -- and feels "betrayed" by -- the disparity between
her lifestyle and her belief of how life should be. She
wonders if in her own way she is as corrupt as Braggioni.
Her belief that "any kind of death" is preferable to being
a traitor to her cause foreshadows her dream of Eugenio.
He offers to show her "a new country . . . far away," to
take her with him to the land of death. That she must
first eat of the Judas tree suggests that even death may be
another betrayal.

DOROTHY PARKER

You Were Perfectly Fine

(p. 518)

"You Were Perfectly Fine" is an excellent study in technique. The author gives us no background and little description of the characters -- not even voice inflections. Yet in only three pages of dialogue she is able to introduce several interesting conflicts which engage our imagination.

The conversation between the "pale young man" and the "clear-eyed girl" is pervaded with irony and innuendo. The irony stems from the fact that much more is being communicated than what is actually being said. Ostensibly the young woman is assuring the young man that he has nothing to worry about, that his behavior the night before was not obnoxious. He was, according to her account, perfectly fine, amusing, wonderful, funny, and absolutely all right. She also manages to note in passing that he almost started a fight, insulted Elinor, sang loudly for an hour, was rude to the waiter, and obnoxious to the old man with white hair. If this were all, we might see the story simply as the young woman's attempt to make the man feel foolish under the guise of being comforting and reassuring.

This story takes a new twist, however, when the woman introduces the "lovely long ride" in the taxi during which Peter talked -- or so she claims -- of his soul and of how he felt about her. She insists that he must remember the ride, that she couldn't bear it, that it would simply kill her if he didn't. He acknowledges the ride and is informed that "it was the most important thing that ever happened" to them. The ensuing comment suggests that the woman believes -- or pretends to believe -- that Peter has made some commitment to her, perhaps proposed marriage. "We're

going to be so happy," she tells a very confused and hung-
over Peter. The phrases sound slightly contrived and self-
serving. The reader may begin to wonder whether perhaps a
great deal of what she has previously said wasn't equally
slanted to suit her own ends.

Parker does not resolve the problem for us. Instead
she adds a final twist by having the young man ask for a
drink after having refused one a few moments earlier. The
request suggests how much he has been affected by what he
has heard. It also implies, especially in light of his
behavior the previous night, that he lacks self-discipline
and willpower. He asks for a drink even as he claims that
he's "off the stuff for life." Peter's lack of resolve,
his loss of memory, and his need for a drink suggest that
the young woman may be getting much more than she bargained
for. (He observes outright that he feels "a collapse coming
on.") We are left wondering not only if her account is
correct, but if she is really "clear-eyed" after all.

JAMES THURBER

The Secret Life of Walter Mitty

(p. 521)

Thurber published over twenty-seven volumes of short stories, essays, sketches, and reminiscences. His most successful piece is this story which, after its appearance in the New Yorker, has been reprinted often and made into a drama for stage, radio, and screen. The widespread popularity of "The Secret Life of Walter Mitty" is due to its deft, humorous presentation of a phenomenon common to all of us. Although the gulf between the routine of our daily lives and our dreams, fantasies, and desires may not begin to compare to that of the world renowned Commander, surgeon, and marksmen Walter Mitty, we all occasionally seek to escape the mundane through imaginary reverie. Like Mitty we often keep such fantasies secret. (Those who publicize or act on their fantasies run the risk of being considered artistic, insane, or both!)

Thurber's tale is much more carefully structured than students realize on first reading. Each of Mitty's reveries grows out of the commonplace activity he is engaged in. The crush of the traffic on the way to town suggests the fantasy of maneuvering the roaring SN202 through "the worst storm in twenty years of Navy flying"; Mrs. Mitty's mention of Dr. Renshaw and the gloves is the catalyst for Dr. Mitty's life-saving drama in the operating room; thoughts of his arm in a sling and the newspaperboy's shouting about the Waterbury trial lead to the image of Mitty as "the greatest pistol shot in the world." Ocassionaly Mitty's fantasies lead him back to reality; "You miserable cur!" jolts his memory and reminds him to buy some puppy biscuit. Even his isolation becomes a heroic act in his war-hero fantasy

when Captain Mitty tells the sergeant to put the co-pilot
to bed with the others: "I'll fly alone."

Despite or perhaps because of his own personal
misfortunes, such as losing one eye in childhood and going
blind in his forties, Thurber was able to write with insight
and humor of the ordinary, unaggressive, modern man.
Walter Mitty escapes the bullying of his wife, the policeman,
and parking attendant by creating his own fantasy world.
As the final firing-squad fantasy suggests, these imaginative
reveries are what saves Mitty. They allow him to remain --
or at least feel -- "undefeated, inscrutable to the last."

F. SCOTT FITZGERALD

Babylon Revisited

(p. 525)

By beginning and ending the story with Charlie at the Ritz, Fitzgerald provides a framework which emphasizes the extreme importance Charlie's past plays in his present attempt to lead a conventional life. Although the Ritz, like Charlie, has changed, it still has connotations which remind us of Charlie's expensive, exuberant lifestyle three years before. Between these framing scenes Fitzgerald deftly creates a sense of the excesses of Parisian life in the old days by having Charlie constantly compare the people and atmosphere he encounters with what he recalls of the past. Much of the time Charlie observes and evaluates the city in terms of what is missing. The difference between the old Charlie and the new is emphasized by the sharp contrast between the Paris he left and the one he returns to. But the difference is not as great as Charlie might have hoped. There is much of Paris and of Charlie that remained unchanged. His sense of the past pervades the present. He takes his daughter to Le Grand Vatel because it is "the only restaurant he could think of not reminiscent of champagne dinners and long luncheons that began at two and ended in a blurred and vague twilight." His own irresponsible past is Charlie's real opponent in his struggle to regain his daughter. Fitzgerald creates suspense and conveys the tension of a lengthy ordeal by repeatedly moving from the domestic dialogue scenes at the Peters' to Charlie's solitary reflections as he encounters familiar landmarks around Paris.

In the person of Marion Peters, Charlie is faced with a constant reminder of past mistakes. Unlike her husband, Marion has no desire to see Charlie as he is now or to reevaluate him as a father. She has an emotional investment in holding fast to her opinion of what he was, of what he did to her sister and, indirectly, to her. Although Marion's hostility is not completely unwarranted, Fitzgerald clearly lets us see that much of it is based on her own resentment toward life, her "discouragement of ill health and adverse circumstances," and jealousy. She sees that Charlie has reformed, but she has lived too long with this prejudice to let it go easily.

Although the appearance of Charlie's old drinking buddies may appear contrived to some readers, it nevertheless emphasizes the truth that Charlie is not completely free of his past. He is no longer the irresponsible heavy drinker of three years ago, but neither is he as relaxed and in control as he would like to appear. Marion's accusations strike sensitive nerves and send "an electric current of agony" through him. As the last sentence suggests, Charlie is in Paris not only because of his love for Honoria and his strong sense of family and responsibility, but also because of a deep sense of loneliness. Fitzgerald shows us enough of Charlie's struggle and insecurity to let us know that, although reformed, Charlie is not free.

WILLIAM FAULKNER

A Rose for Emily

(p. 540)

In many of Faulkner's novels and short stories, the values, traditions, beliefs, and mistakes of the past play a major role in shaping the lives of the those in the present. The past, as Faulkner once remarked, isn't dead. For some, such as Miss Emily Grierson, it is more alive than the present. She closes her doors on the modern world, rejects "improvements" such as a mailbox or metal numbers above her door, and, in the narrator's words, clings "to that which had robbed her, as people will." Her father's aristocratic sense of superiority, his feeling that none of the young men were quite good enough for his daughter, robbed Emily of the chance for a normal life with a husband and a family. When he dies, she clings to her past and demands "more than ever the recognition of her dignity as the last Grierson."

Faulkner heightens our sense of the influence and ever-present quality of the past through his unusual method of presenting Emily's life. Beginning with her death in the twentieth century, we move back to 1894 when Colonel Sartoris remitted her taxes, forward a whole generation in paragraph four when the younger men have become city authorities, back thirty years to an account of the smell, back two years further to her father's death, forward to her romance with Homer Barron, then to her later years, the china-painting episode, her death, and the final revelation. The unusual juxtaposition underscores Faulkner's view that the past and present are inextricably intertwined.

The gothic revelation of the final paragraphs allows Faulkner to vividly drive home his view of the high price one pays for living in the past. Figuratively and literally,

Miss Emily has been living among the dead. Even her body looks like something preserved in formaldehyde, "bloated, like a body long submerged in motionless water."

Yet Faulkner is by no means rejecting the past in favor of "progress." The author is not interested in praising one generation over another but in pointing out the virtues and failings of both. He describes Miss Emily's decaying house, for example, surrounded by cotton wagons and gasoline pumps, as "an eyesore among eyesores." He makes clear in the story of Miss Emily's taxes and the divided town council meeting concerning the smell, that there are qualities, such as respect and politeness, which are not found as readily in the younger generations. Despite her possible insanity, there is a strength of character and an independence in Miss Emily which is not found among the gossipy, nosey townspeople. The narrative voice, the "we" of the tale, is not that of an individual or even a generation. It is the view of the town over many years. Through it Faulkner gives us a revealing account of the interest and envy the townspeople felt toward the "high and mighty Griersons."

WILLIAM FAULKNER

That Evening Sun

(p. 547)

Though the Compsons are featured in The Sound and the Fury, both Mr. Compson and Quentin appear as narrators in Absalom, Absalom!, and Nancy survives as Nancy Mannigoe in Requiem for a Nun, bringing these related contexts to "That Evening Sun" diminishes the independent achievement of Faulkner's story and robs it of its thematic impact. To know that Nancy survives, for instance, might cause us to dismiss her terror as the product of an overactive imagination, thus lessening Faulkner's indictment of the Compsons for not seeing Nancy through what he terms the "crisis of her need" in Faulkner in the University. Quentin's narration would likewise lose its economical impact if overburdened with the weight of Faulkner's other novels.

While Nancy is the ostensible protagonist, one might make a strong case for Quentin as the main focus of the story. The gap of fifteen years between the events and the narration, and the foreboding contrast between the present and the past seem to promise an in-depth study of both Nancy and social change, but the story quickly becomes an objective chronicle of the Compsons' relationship with Nancy. Even Quentin's childhood reactions to the events rarely find their way into the narration, which concentrates on studying the interactions of the characters and building up dramatic tension.

The brief incident between Nancy and Mr. Stovall is crucial to understanding the story's theme. Sexually used by Stovall, Nancy manages to indict him as she is being taken to jail, but in the process she loses not only her teeth but also her hold on her identity. "I ain't nothing but a nigger," Nancy continues to assert as her sense of self-worth gradually crumbles; the only consolation she can grasp is that in her powerlessness, she is not at fault. Mr. Compson exhibits understanding attempts to help Nancy through her plight; he cannot hold out, however, against his wife's callous self-centeredness and finally relinquishes responsibility for his laundress's safety.

The Compson children, who are characterized very distinctly, stand in the middle of this drama, drawn in by Nancy's strange behavior and the change it causes in their household. Caddy is distinguished by her precocious sexual curiosity, her bending of the rules, and her daring. Jason, the youngest, uses the situation as an opportunity to manipulate the others, to attempt to prove himself their equal, and finally to achieve his own ends by tattling. Quentin, though seemingly detached, has the most acute perceptions -- visual, olfactory, and intellectual. His final question ("Who will do our washing now, Father?") suggests an understanding that Nancy's fear of death may become a reality. The lingering uncertainty about Nancy's fate, however, has the effect of shifting the focus of the drama to the twilight of the Compson family and the intrusion of these events into the world of childhood.

ERNEST HEMINGWAY

A Clean, Well-Lighted Place

(p. 559)

When asked to name the protagonist of this story, students
may be unsure whether the story centers on the old man in
the café or the older waiter. Although the old man is
turned out into the street halfway through the story, he
remains in the old waiter's mind. The two are kindred
spirits, and we learn about one through the other; thus
these two representatives of the older generation might be
seen as complementary protagonists. Deaf but sensitive to
the absence of commotion around him, the old man finds a
welcome sense of order and personal dignity in drinking in a
clean, well-lighted café. His failed suicide attempt, we
learn from the waiters, is not the result of simple monetary
problems; since no explicit cause is named, we are left to
construct for ourselves the dark sources of his despair.

The girl and the soldier do not appear fortuitously in
Hemingway's economical story. Unlike the old man, the
soldier lives in a world which certain rules are rigidly
enforced; if he is out after curfew, he will be picked up
by the guards. For the old man, no such superior force
imposes a scheme of order on the universe. As the older
waiter recognizes, his nightly retreat into drunkenness in
the clean, well-lighted café temporarily arrests the sense
of meaninglessness he perceives so strongly in a dark,
uncertain world.

The younger waiter fails to understand the old man's
continued presence at the café; when he refills the old
man's brandy, he makes abusive comments and overflows the
glass, violating his sense of cleanliness and perhaps hoping
such rudeness will drive him away. The older waiter, on

the other hand, respects the old man's cleanliness and understands his need to seek the light of the café -- the community of those lonely and alienated souls who no longer feel fear and dread but sense that "It was all a nothing and a man was nothing too." The parodies of the "Our Father" and the "Hail Mary" comment on the ineffectuality of religion as a comfort in such a world; yet the parodies become prayers in their own right for the waiter, who uses the old forms as an expression of the faith he shares with those for whom the clean, well-lighted café has replaced the church.

JORGE LUIS BORGES

The Babylon Lottery

Translated by Emece Editores, S.A.

(p. 563)

Borges's short stories often force us to examine carefully
events or beliefs which at first glance do not appear
particularly extraordinary or even interesting. Commonplace
attitudes and assumptions are made to appear marvelous,
bizarre, and even terrifying. One reason for his success
in "The Babylon Lottery" is that he discusses the role of
chance in unusual terms, using the language of the theologian,
the occultist, the historian, the mathematician, and the
scientist. There is mention of "the sacred scriptures,"
the "council of wizards," the "new order . . . a necessary
historical stage," the "discussions of a juridico-mathematical
nature," and the "giratory spheres." (Students should be
encouraged to discuss the effect of such language as well
as the meanings of other unusual words used in this story:
pusillanimous, ecclesiastical, metaphysical, sacerdotal,
eponymous, paleographic, heresiarch.)

    While claiming no intimate knowledge of the mysteries
of the lottery or its history, the narrator carefully
describes how the nature of the lottery changes from a game
whose "moral virtue was nil" to something much more profound.
The most significant change is what the narrator terms "a
slight reform: the interpolation of a certain small number
of adverse outcomes among the favored numbers." Once this
change is effected the lottery takes on a very different
moral quality. Soon peer pressure and the removal of
monetary barriers and rewards result in widespread
participation: "The Babylonians gave themselves up to the
game." Just as Babylon was the place of captivity for the
Jews in the Old Testament, so the narrator's Babylon is a

place of captivity for those who give the Company power over their "intimate hopes and intimate terrors." Once the Company has assumed complete public power its workings become increasingly secret, mysterious, and sacred. It is no longer a human organization. The narrator compares the Company to God and notes that its workings gave rise "to all manner of conjectures." For some, the Company is omnipotent, while for others it is only a fantasy which has never existed. Students should be asked to draw parallels between "The Babylon Lottery" and the role of mystery, chance, and fate in our lives. Are things more certain or less ambiguous for us than for the narrator? The narrator suggests the subjective nature of reality not only by including opposing views but by admitting that his own account is falsified in some degree.

SEAN O'FAOLAIN

The Man Who Invented Sin

(p. 568)

Sean O'Faolain prides himself on being an Irish writer. He
has remarked that he prefers to think of every writer as
writing from a particular national perspective or, as he
puts it, "dyed Irish, English, French, German, Greek,
Indian. . . ." "The Man Who Invented Sin" is filled with
references to the Irish countryside, its mountains, bogs,
and lakes as well as the traditional human activities there:
"dances, moonlight boating paties, singsongs in the cottages."
Into this setting comes a traditional Irish institution,
Irish Catholicism. O'Faolain does an excellent job of
showing the subtle yet powerful influence of this
environment on the two young monks and two nuns who lodge
at Mrs. Ryder's. The narrator tells us that there was
"nothing remarkable" about the four students. But what
happens to them is remarkable. Once taken out of the
strict pattern of hostel life and forced to live in close
proximity, they begin to see each other as individual human
beings, not simply as servants of the church. They also
begin to come under the sway of their surroundings.

O'Faolain resists the temptation to tell his story
directly. Instead he gives us vivid descriptions of
particular incidents, such as Majellan consoling Magdalen
in the hallway or Virgilius teaching the others pitch and
toss, which allow us to see the metamorphoses taking place.
(This is perhaps one reason why a dramatic adaptation of
"The Man Who Invented Sin" was broadcast in England in 1970.)
So smoothly does O'Faolain ease us into accepting the new
identities of the four -- a process which, appropriately
enough, is accompanied by new names -- that we, too, are

shocked by the dramatic entrance of Lispeen as Maggie and
Jelly are trying to learn to waltz. There are hints, later
confirmed, that the curate is simply overacting a role.
Nevertheless his actions have a marked effect on the four
young people. They are now unified by opposition and their
escapades become even more daring. The narrator shrewdly
remarks that the "Serpent had come into the garden with the
most wily of temptations." He questions whether they are
entirely at ease with their new-found freedom. Guilt may
have been a fifth companion on all of their excursions.
They have learned their lessons too well to disregard them
completely. "Time ceases to exist on a lake," the narrator
notes accurately. Yet it begins again in earnest when the
four return from their final night's excursion on the boat
to confront the "black figure" on the causeway. Majellan's
change of heart reflects the truth of his statement that
"it's not good to take people out of their rut. I didn't
enjoy that summer." We know, of course, that he enjoyed it
more than he admits; what he doesn't enjoy is having enjoyed
it. The paradox of freedom and restraint in the Irish
Catholic religion is foreshadowed in O'Faolain's delicate
descriptions of the widely varying moods of the Irish
landscape and country life. The gaiety of the folk-song
concert in the garden and the surreptitious boating parties
on the mountain lake is only one view. The narrator also
sees the "melancholy filmy light" of the night landscape
when the houses are "black and silent." And the mountain
itself echoes the words of the black figure on the shore.

NATHALIE SARRAUTE

Tropism XVIII

Translated by Maria Jolas

(p. 577)

With its lack of action and plot, this story provides an
excellent opportunity to discuss the nature of the modern
short story. Undoubtedly, some students will not consider
"Tropism XVIII" a story at all. A discussion of their
reasons may help them form a set of critical guidelines to
aid their reading of other stories in the collection. The
story comes from Sarraute's book Tropisms, in which she
tries to eschew the standard literary conventions of clearly
defined plot, character, and conflict in order to capture
"those hidden dramatic actions, those tropisms."
    As in William Carlos Williams's "The Red Wheelbarrow,"
we are given only minimal information, which is not
interpreted. Its value must be determined by the reader.
(Students may debate the value of leaving out so much of
the tale.) They may reject this story, as they often do
Williams's poem on first reading, as not representative of
the genre. The brevity of both works forces the reader to
examine closely what is given. Each minute detail is
important. We are told the material the curtains are made
of and yet are not told the name of the white-haired lady.
Despite its brevity, the story does leave us with a very
definite sense of this stiff spinster with pink and purple
cheeks and her "little universe." Regardless of their
final opinion of "Tropism XVIII," students have been
compelled to take a hard, close look at a rather commonplace
scene. Because of that achievement alone, Sarraute, like
Williams, can be considered successful.

JOHN STEINBECK ================

Flight

(p. 578)

In the short story "Flight," first published in the collection
The Long Valley, Steinbeck focuses on the fate of a young
Californian paisano, one of the lowly whose lives provide
the fabric of most of this writer's work. The story has a
strongly Wild-Western flavor and the presentation is highly
cinematic. The reliance on vivid descriptive passages and
dialogue makes for an almost balladlike movement in the
development of the plot. Although it can be viewed as the
tale of a boy's initiation into manhood, there is no sense
of a process or of a developing consciousness, and the
young man's maturity is tragically brief. The clipped
sparseness of Steinbeck's style, reminiscent of Hemingway,
corresponds to the simple, harsh lives he describes, and in
spite of the almost dispassionate bluntness of the diction,
the story conveys a sense of pity and understanding. Pepé
is never viewed as a murderer, never blamed: his knife
"went almost by itself."
        The tragic dénouement is predictable from the moment
we see Pepé's dexterity with his father's knife. The weapon
symbolizes manhood, but it is ironic that this inheritance
comes to Pepé in a purely destructive way. A sense of
fatalism is consistently present. In the story Mama Torres's
husband is bitten in the chest by a rattlesnake and "there
is not much that can be done." Her strength in facing the
results of Pepé's crime indicates the same attitude toward
life. The fugitive's developing manhood and survival
instinct is counteracted by the spreading gangrene of his
wound. Significantly, the story concludes with the image
of the avalanche, underlining the irresistible force of

circumstance. This naturalistic vision is evident from the opening descriptive paragraph, where environmental forces seem hostile to man: the ocean hisses, the barn is bitten by the sea salt, the slope is "sterile" and the farm buildings are mere "clinging aphids."

Toward the end of the story the point of view becomes more and more confined to Pepé's perceptions. His isolation in a hard-bitten natural environment is thus so intensely conveyed that his death comes almost as a relief.

FRANK O'CONNOR ========

Guests of the Nation

(p. 590)

Frank O'Connor is the pseudonymn of Irish writer Michael
O'Donovan, who was a member of the Irish Republican Army
during the Irish Civil War -- the period in which the story
"Guests of the Nation" is set. O'Connor's delicate management
of the first-person narration conveys that strong sense of
a veritable personal voice which he always strove to achieve.
It is familiar enough to draw the reader easily into the
conflicts of the period and the lives of the characters,
colloquial enough to have an Irish flavor, but flexible and
lyrical enough to modulate into the beautifully poetic
concluding paragraph. The ironic euphemism of the title
refers to two English prisoners captured by the IRA and
left in the rather friendly custody of two young soldiers
with the heroic names of Bonaparte and Noble. The implications
of this cliche are revitalized when the young Irishmen are
given the duty of executing the "guests," who also have claims
to their loyalty as "chums." The theme of conflicting
loyalties, duties, and responsiblities is central to the
story. Although the perverseness of such "duties" that
force a man to shoot men whom he knows and likes is made
painfully evident, Belcher's dignified acceptance of his
fate and his refusal to blame anyone focus one's attention
on the sheer human tragedy more than on the injustice of
the events. "I never could make out what duty was myself
. . . I think you are all good lads, if that's what you mean.
I'm not complaining." One may recall O'Connor's remark
that "storytelling is the nearest thing one can get to the
quality of pure lyric poem . . . It doesn't deal with
problems; it doesn't have any solutions to offer; it just
states the human condition."

The story benefits greatly from the sensitive characterization of the Englishmen, the quiet Belcher and the voluble Hawkins. The latter's character is largely revealed through his excessive "old gab" and his energetic arguments with Noble which, as becomes evident, are an expression of friendship. Belcher shows a simple and moving dignity in his actions and self-revelation toward the end. The grief of the old Irish woman whom he treated with such politeness and of his "hosts" is thus readily shared by the reader.

≡ ISAAC BASHEVIS SINGER

The Beard

*Translated by Isaac Bashevis Singer
and Herbert R. Lottman*

(p. 599)

In an interview for the journal <u>Commentary</u>, Isaac Bashevis
Singer, Yiddish author and Nobel Prize Winner, explained
why he chose to be a writer instead of a rabbi like his
ancestors: ". . . I very often met situations which baffled
me, and from the moment I knew there was such a thing as
literature, I thought how wonderful it would be to be able
to describe such things." This sense that literature deals
with life's strangeness and uncertainty is evoked by the
words of the bearded Mrs. Pupko -- recalled by the narrator
at the very end of the story: "<u>Nu</u>, one mustn't know
everything." (The same idea, instilled perhaps in the
Jewish mind by the Book of Job, is evident in Bernard
Malamud's story "The Jewbird" when the crow says: "Who
knows? . . . Does God tell us everything?")
       Mrs. Pupko's beard, strange and disconcerting on a
woman, seems even more so to the narrator at the end of the
story. The fact that she has not shaved it off after her
husband's death draws into question her story that she
grew it only to please him, and, by extension, the whole
sad tale about the narrator's involvement in Pupko's
deterioration, which has caused him to revoke his resolve
never to write about the man. The question of whether the
narrator was subject to deliberate emotional blackmail
remains unresolved. It seems likely that he was, but the
many mysteries surrounding Pupko and his wife prevent
narrator and reader from deciding the issue unambiguously:
"People have idiosyncrasies," as the bearded woman says,
"which cannot be explained by theories." Singer is a
storyteller, not a psychologist, and declared as much in

his Commentary interview: "When I tell a story, I tell a story. I don't try to discuss, criticize, or analyze my characters."

The story also takes a wry look at the position of a somewhat cliquish literary set -- Yiddish, moreover -- in relation to American capitalist society. Singer, who once said, "I am still surprised every time I get a check for a story," and yet achieved fame and financial success, probably identifies in some measure with both the narrator and Pupko. After all, the latter's work, like Singer's, includes "half-crazed people, chronic misers, old country quarrels . . ." Pupko's financial success at first seems unbelievable to the unworldly writers, as does the fact that an eminent critic can be bought. The ironic twist in the plot is that the narrator, despite his protestations, also is finally bought by subtle psychological means which include, certainly, his embarassment at having his neighbors see him with the monstrous Mrs. Pupko. Society thus asserts its pressures through social as well as financial means.

RICHARD WRIGHT

The Man Who
Killed a Shadow

(p. 605)

In this story, as in his finest novels, <u>Native Son</u> and
<u>Black Boy</u>, Wright examines the segregated world of the
South from the perspective of an uneducated black man. The
story vividly captures the sense of unreality that haunts
Saul as he grows up feeling like a "black island" amid a
sea of white faces. His poverty, his frequent moves to a
series of dirty little towns, increased his sense of
isolation. His homes lacked any emotional meaning for the
boy, and the people in his town "really never became
personalities" to him before he was forced to move on.
Even his brothers and sisters remained strangers to him.
The narrator writes that by the age of twelve all of reality
appeared to Saul as a series of names without substance.
The world appears a "vast shadow-world" controlled by unseen
forces.

Once he is an adult, engaged in menial jobs that demand
little personality or intelligence, Saul begins to focus
his anxieties and fears upon the white shadow-world. He
outwardly accepts his inferior status, but he does not feel
inferior. As his sense of alienation or unreality increases,
Saul turns to whisky as the only thing which could make
his world appear "more reasonably three-dimensional."

Whisky is no defense, however, against the unexpected
sexual overtures of the petite blond librarian. Wright
here draws several distinct, unsettling parallels between
racism and sex and violence. Society treats Saul as a
person without individual emotions and aspirations; the
librarian approaches him coldly and impersonally. He does
not even know her name when she calls him over to clean

under her desk. The woman's treatment of Saul as both a
servant and sex object is doubly demeaning to him as a
human being. His unpremeditated violence toward her appears
to be the release of the anger and hostility which has its
roots in the distant past. Her murder is in this sense as
impersonal as her treatment of this "black nigger" with
whom she wants to have intercourse. The violent, impersonal
nature of the murder, and of racial prejudice, is underscored
by the concluding medical report. She has not been raped;
there is only the violent, impersonal penetration of the
knife in her throat.

EUDORA WELTY

Why I Live at the P.O.

(p. 614)

The story's title indicates that what follows will be an individual's explanation -- perhaps self-justification -- for her unusual place of residence. Very early in the story the narrator refutes her sister's claim that she is "one-sided. Bigger on one side than the other, which is a deliberate, calculated falsehood: I'm the same." Whatever her proportions, however, we should sense that the narrator's tale will be somewhat one-sided, since she is obviously upset over her spoiled younger sister's theft of Mr. Whitaker ("the only man ever dropped down in China Grove") and subsequent speedy return to the shelter of her family. Stella-Rondo, like the Prodigal Son in the Biblical parable, is welcomed back into the family with full exoneration; however, no such smooth resolution of sibling jealousy occurs in this story.

   Students might consider how Stella-Rondo would relate these incidents in order to understand the narrator's particular slant on events more completely. As Papa-Daddy comments, Stella-Rondo at least "deserved credit for getting out of town," though she had ulterior motives for her sudden exit from China Grove. The narrator, on the other hand, settles into a niche as the postmistress of the "next to smallest P.O. in the state of Mississippi" and the unappreciated, long-suffering daughter in a bizarre and unpredictable family. Although Stella does artfully succeed in turning the family against her, the narrator is hardly the martyr she makes herself out to be. Nonetheless, she is the only one in the family who will face up to the unpleasant truth that Shirley-T's amazing resemblance to

104

Papa-Daddy is more than coincidental. While the family
consistently upholds the fiction that Shirley-T is an
adopted child, the narrator relentlessly persists in exposing
their pretense; she even intimates that Shirley-T may be
retarded since she has not spoken (a possible result of
inbreeding), but her mother attempts to explain away any
such possibility with Mr. Whitaker's drinking.

The response to the narrator's challenge -- Shirley-
T's less than profound "baby-talk" -- is only one indication
of the pervasive satire of these rural Mississippians which
Welty has embedded in her narrator's comic monologue. The
haphazard information about her family which the narrator
delivers in an almost deadpan tone (e.g. "Pappa-Daddy's
Mama's papa and sulks" and Stella "pulling out every one of
her eyebrows with some cheap Kress tweezers") only intensifies
the caricature. We laugh at the characters' foibles when
Uncle Rondo drunkenly parades around in Stella's kimono and
at their limitations when we hear about their childish
behavior (which the narrator is not exempt from).

Still, balancing the many sources of comedy that elicit
a type of humorous tolerance is an awareness of a more
vindictive undercurrent which tinges even the narrator's
haphazard remarks. Even though the narrator indulges in
pettiness and instigation of her own, the sense of persecution
she feels is real, and her retreat to the P.O. becomes an
index of her growing alienation. In her five-day sojourn
at the P.O., she sets up "everything cater-cornered, the
way I like it" and finds temporary peace, even though it is
through an armistice which closes down the town's means of
communication with the outside world.

The Swimmer

(p. 623)

The greatest difficulty for the reader of "The Swimmer" should not be with the shifts from omniscient narration to Neddy Merrill's consciousness but with the shifting time frame. The story begins as a realistic recounting of a single day's swim; Neddy very clearly lays out the course of his pilgrimage, and his course down the "Lucinda River," as he names it, does follow this initial sequence exactly. Students should note that the turning point of the narrative occurs when Neddy takes shelter from the storm in the Levys' gazebo. At first, it seems as if the chill Neddy feels after the rain arises from the cooling effect of the storm, and as if the maple leaves on the ground are victims of a midsummer blight. Yet these details, which are immediately reinforced by the scenes of the Lindleys' overgrown riding ring and the Welchers' dry pool, quickly take on a figurative meaning. They signal a passage of time, and change the initially realistic narrative into a telescoped journey in which the no-longer-youthful Neddy swims through the wake of his personal and financial misfortunes. As we follow Neddy's swim, we piece together his repressed past along with him and realize that he can no longer swim back to the home he inhabited so nonchalantly at the beginning of his initial plunge.

Neddy's swim is not begun as an escape from a boring life of wealth, comfort, and parties; instead it represents an indulgence in the pleasures of that life -- a midsummer indulgence which takes him away from his family and friends until he begins his quest in search of them during his autumn years. Once Neddy leaves the waterways of his exclusive neighborhood, he is no longer insulated and must make a "difficult portage" across the public realm. Stranded in the middle of traffic on Route 424, Neddy becomes subject to the ridicule and abuse of social traffic: swimming the public pool, he must follow society's rules even though he has no ready identity in this world. What was begun as a quest for personal fulfillment and diversion has turned into the unpleasant discovery that change is cruel and inevitable.

Neddy's attempts to discover some sustenance and consolation in the final stretch of his journey prove increasingly ineffectual and debilitating. At the Hallorans', he is confronted with reminders of personal misfortune and the passage of time. Next, Eric Sachs provides a brief symbolic counterpart of Neddy's condition; the scars from his surgery leave him no trace of a navel, "no link to birth" -- figuratively cut off from human community. The visit to the Biswangers' brings home Neddy's former snobbery and his loss of status when he meets with financial misfortune. At his age, as his visit to Shirley demonstrates, the "supreme elixir" of sex no longer provides its former consolations. His vigor sapped by the journey, Neddy does swim home, only to find the past locked away from him and empty, an unavailable shelter from the storm.

RALPH ELLISON

Flying Home

(p. 631)

Ellison's masterpiece is his 1952 novel <u>Invisible Man</u>, which was selected by literary critics in 1965 as the most distinguished novel published since World War II. In it Ellison movingly explores the trials and betrayals of a young black man who attempts to rise in a white world. "Flying Home" also presents the sense of isolation and the need for community experienced by a black man who seeks to escape the traditional roles and lifestyles adopted by or forced upon those of his race. Todd realizes that he is different from most other blacks in his world, separated from them "by age, by understanding, by sensibility, by technology and by his need to measure himself against the mirror of other's men's appreciation." His desire to be more, to be different, is appropriately symbolized by his desire to fly. Traditionally, in literature and mythology flying is the symbol of freedom and imagination. Several times in the story Ellison uses flight as a metaphor for Todd's life. His course of flight has led him away "from all needed and natural landmarks." He is no longer a part of the familiar, comforting world he once knew. Neither is he able to trust his white colleagues. He feels caught between "ignorant black men and condescending whites." His isolation and rebellion are reflected in his occupation as a military pilot flying alone. The accident, which leaves him helpless and in extreme pain, reflects his emotional and psychological states. Todd realizes that he is at fault for his accident. He "had been flying too high and too fast." He had been done in by a buzzard, which as the story progresses, comes to symbolize his roots in the

black community. Initially, he resents the old man's story
of his trip to heaven. Even in heaven blacks are kept in
harness and not allowed to achieve their full potential.
Todd's reaction to Jefferson's flying story defines his own
attitude toward flying and the black community: "Maybe we
are a bunch of buzzards feeding on a dead horse, but we can
hope to be eagles, can't we?" By the end of the story,
after his confrontation with the callous Mr. Graves, Todd
experiences a new awareness of his bond with other black
men who have suffered as he has. He is no longer ashamed
of Jefferson but begins to laugh as he did and look to
him as his "sole salvation in an insane world of outrage
and humiliation." The final sentence, in which the buzzard
becomes a bird of flaming gold, reflects Todd's new
understanding and acceptance of himself as a black man. He
realizes that true freedom is found not in accomplishment
but in community. The "new current of communication"
between Todd and Jefferson and the boy lifts him "out of
his isolation, back into the world of men."

BERNARD MALAMUD

The Jewbird

(p. 643)

In this story by the American Jewish writer Bernard Malamud, the matter-of-fact tone and brisk narration emphasize, by contrast, the cartoon-like unreality of the plot and the double-edged criticism of the attitude of "insiders" toward "outsiders."

Schwartz, the crow, bears an appropriate and typically Jewish name; indeed, he is archetypically Jewish in his humor, his language, his customs -- in all except for the bizarre fact that he happens to be a bird. He is -- as a scavenger, a "black," and a Jew -- an outsider, temporarily and begrudgingly let in by the New York Cohen family. His bedraggled appearance and first words ("Gevalt, a pogrom!") recall the tragic history of the Jewish diaspora and persecution, of which he is emblematic.

Cohen, who wants to keep the crow out, expects him to be migratory, and sees him as a freeloader who is ugly and smelly (the standard complaint of the racially prejudiced). The fact that Schwartz in fact makes modest demands and helps Maurie Cohen with his homework in comically avuncular fashion does nothing to relieve Cohen's stubborn resentment of the intruder. Cohen himself is "Jewish" in his solidly middle-class existence as a frozen foods salesman and in his ambitions to become more of an "insider" -- ambitions revealed in his unrealistic dream of an Ivy League career for his son. The central irony of the tale is that it is the Jew himself who makes the Jewbird a scapegoat. When his mother dies and Maurie gets a zero on an arithmetic test, Cohen violently ejects the bird, thus demonstrating the irrational allocation of blame that lies at the heart of anti-Semitism and racism. When the kindly Edie, at the conclusion of the story, lays the blame for Schwartz's death (in the bird's own accents) on "Anti-Semeets," she unconsciously condemns her own husband. Moreover, by laying the blame on "the others," she is also guilty of failing to realize that a lack of charity toward the outsider could render the Jew no different from his persecutors.

The ending contains a deft ambiguity: it remains unclear whether Cohen actually killed the bird or simply broke his heart. The latter interpretation seems more likely. This allows one to assume that the sad fable of Schwartz and Cohen could have been repeated in yet another context. The anonymity of the "dead black bird" and the touch of mystery surrounding his violent end stress the universality of this parable.

SAUL BELLOW

Looking for Mr. Green

(p. 650)

In his determined search for Mr. Green, George Grebe seems
to be guided by the injunction from Ecclesiastes which
serves as the story's epigraph. No longer idle, he carries
out his job with the intensity of a hunter, dispensing
relief checks to those who are unable to pick them up.
Grebe's job provides him with a similar economic relief, as
well as with a sense of purpose. Still, he realizes that
his service, unlike that of his parents, was one "which no
visible asked for, and probably flesh and blood could not
even perform. Nor could anyone show why it should be
performed; or see where the performance would lead." For
his job to have meaning and fulfillment, Grebe must determine
them as he carries out his seemingly futile task. Thus,
looking for Mr. Green becomes a quest for some affirmation
of reality, a theme which Raynor's comments and Grebe's
reflections near the end of the story bring out into the
open.

Grebe's morning interview with Raynor reveals the
extent of Grebe's education as well as the differences in
the two men's beliefs. The Latin quotations they trade
illustrate their respective positions well: Raynor's maxims
("While there's life there's hope" and "The die is cast")
are somewhat more resigned than Grebe's ("Give your hand to
the wretched" and "Ever upwards"), which suggest action and
direction. Grebe assesses Raynor favorably, but receives
little guidance from his supervisor; Raynor, in fact, seems
to make Grebe's mission more difficult (and somewhat more
absurd) by not encouraging preparation and by treating the
job so casually.

Other characters Grebe encounters on his quest also
provide significant attitudes toward existence which affect
his perspective. Mrs. Staika's tirade against the fakes
on the relief roles may initially cause some doubt about
Mr. Green's existence, but her noisy presence gives Grebe a
sense of the struggle in his district -- "the war of flesh
and blood" -- which the relief checks at least continue.
Grebe recoils from the Italian grocer's nightmare vision of
the ghetto as a realm of fluid identity and senseless crime;
he cannot accept that this vision is one to which others
would give consent. Mr. Field's visionary scheme of creating
black millionaires -- Platonic ideals for their race --
becomes more tantalizing as Grebe's search for Mr. Green
continues, because Grebe understands that both involve belief
without absolute confirmation.

Mr. Green continually recedes from Grebe as he draws
closer to his goal. Although he delivers the check to a
drunken, naked woman who neither affirms nor denies that
she is Mrs. Green, Grebe understands, in the final assertion
that Green "could be found," that he must make some leap of
faith; like those who pay to ride on the El, he must consent
to accept appearance in order to keep things running smoothly.
"Nothing was deliberately hidden," Grebe believes before he
begins his search, and he affirms this truth in his quest
for Mr. Green, who remains beyond his touch, but not because
of any deliberate scheme to frustrate man in his quest to
penetrate the world of appearances.

CARSON McCULLERS ═══════════

A Tree, a Rock, a Cloud

(p. 664)

The opening paragraph effectively sets the tone for this
story. To escape the rain and the "raw, empty street," the
boy goes into the streetcar café for a cup of coffee. He
encounters a rather unsociable, uncommunicative group of
soldiers, spinners, the "bitter and stingy" owner, and the
old man. No one talks or even looks at him until he is on
his way out. It is an effective beginning because it is
this very coldness that the old man wants to talk about.
How does one love in a world where love is often not returned
or even recognized? The café regulars view the old man as
a momentary diversion and greet his conversation with
laughter.

The boy, however, does not laugh. Neither can he pull
away. Like the Ancient Mariner, the old man possesses
"something . . . that held the boy and would not let him
go away." The man attempts to explain his past experiences
and his quest to understand the nature of love. He has
learned that one must begin with not self-centered sexual
love, but with a selfless love for all of nature. Beginning
with a tree, a rock, a cloud, one can progress to loving a
goldfish, a bird, or a street full of people. The
distinguished critic William Rodney Allen writes that
"McCullers was greatly influenced by the ethics of the
philosopher Leibnitz, who believed in a universal rather
than a discriminating love." The old man calls his efforts
to understand a "science" because he has slowly and
methodically built up his knowledge of this mysterious
phenomenon.

In contrast to the old man's sincerity is Leo's crude running commentary. He begins by jeering at the story and finally tells the man to shut up. His attitude toward his customers, and toward the story, reveals the great difference between Leo's concept of self-expression and understanding and that of the old man. Yet, significantly, even Leo refuses to affirm the boy's suggestion that the old man simply may be crazy. Clearly, the tale of the man's quest has made a strong impression on the café owner as well as on the newspaper boy.

ARTHUR C. CLARKE

The Sentinel

(p. 670)

"On the moon," the narrator observes, "there is no loss of detail with distance -- none of that almost imperceptible haziness which softens and sometimes transfigures all far-off things on Earth." The narrator's painstaking descriptions of his immediate surroundings and the lunar landscape create a sense of verisimilitude without which such a science fiction story might be dismissed as implausible. The narrator guides our imagination to a precise point on the Moon and endows that spot with realistic detail that is familiar enough to make the scene sharp in our mind's eye. The almost "homey" environment he sketches shows the astronauts' attempts to impose the familiarity of Earth on the forbidding alien environment.

The most dramatic difference between the lunar landscape and Earth is the absence of life. The "tideless oceans" resemble the primordial seas of Earth, but the lack of life-giving moisture makes the Moon a barren planet which the astronauts futilely explore for signs of life. Its mountains are loftier and seem more forbidding than those on earth until the narrator adjusts the height to a scale commensurate with the gravitational forces. Although the Moon is a "little world" with an "empty heart," the very absence of Earth's visual and cultural limitations makes it the ideal realm for the narrator's discovery.

After he discovers the pyramidal structure, the narrator unsuccessfully attempts to determine its purpose. He is impressed with its smoothness and thrown off by its smallness, but the surrounding force field suggests that this object is not a building or a temple but a machine with no real

meaning in itself. Thus he realizes that the structure is
also another "alien," which yields no secrets about the
Moon itself but will perhaps be the key to greater mysteries.
Wilson's theory about the structure as a sentinel or "fire
alarm" seems more plausible than the discarded theories
which approach its function from a utilitarian perspective.

The sentinel is hardly the traditional object of a
quest; to learn its secret, man must destroy it and discover
that it contains no answers. Its location on the Moon is
significant because to reach it man must have achieved a
certain level of technology and survived its dangers through
intelligence; the narrator characterizes this step as a
"crisis" that has been passed. Appropriately, the discovery
of the sentinel is made in the Mare Crisium (the Sea of
Crises), not the Mare Serenitatis (the Sea of Serenity);
only after emerging from his earthly sea of serenity to the
harsh clarity of crises, Clarke suggests, will man confront
that which is beyond his immediate understanding.

To Room Nineteen

(p. 677)

"To Room Nineteen" has the temporal scope usually reserved
for a novel, but the narrator easily sweeps across nearly
twenty years of the Rawlings' marriage in the first few
pages of the story. Susan and Matthew are presented as a
"balanced and sensible" couple guided by "intelligence" in
their consistent choices of the logical and modern alternative
at every juncture of their marriage. Yet, as the title
indicates, Susan's spiritual movement is toward Room
Nineteen, which comes to represent the inner self that she
puts in abeyance while raising her children. The narrator's
stance, as well as the title, indicates that the surface
calm of the relationship will finally disintegrate when
"intelligence" fails to address the problems at hand.
Students should trace the subtle ways in which the narrator
undercuts "intelligence" in the early part of the story by
portraying how Matthew and Susan often arrive at the
"sensible" alternative by means of rationalization and at
the cost of their emotions.

After years of surrendering to the compelling logic of
self-sacrifice, Susan finds herself unable to enjoy the
freedom that should be her reward when the last of the
children are "off her hands." She cannot logically blame
her condition on her husband, but "their infallible sense
for choosing right" has not translated into a foolproof
formula for living right. Judged solely by the results
(Susan's hallucinations and suicide), their modern,
"intelligent" choices seem no better than the traditional
guidelines which have destroyed their friends' marriages.
Since most of the story is related through Susan's

consciousness, we witness the inner pain and the spiritual death that are the ultimate cost of such control. Certainly the same theme might be conveyed by telling the story from Matthew's point of view, but it is doubtful that Lessing would maintain the same sympathetic slant on his character as she does on Susan's.

Matthew changes very little in the course of the story; he maintains the balance and "abstinence from painful experience" that the couple originally possesses. When Susan fabricates the story about a lover to hide her real motives for going to Room Nineteen, he suggests a foursome as the most logical and least emotionally painful solution to their problems. Yet Susan's true "lover" is the room itself, and the sense of distance it provides from the garden and the "devils of exasperation." Students may be tempted to dismiss the protagonist's condition as mental illness when she begins to see hallucinations, but should observe her consciousness of her plight as well as her purposeful control of her actions. Lessing's paradox, of course, is that highly refined "intelligence" or logic represents one form of madness. Susan's suicide is, unfortunately, the logical resolution of her dilemma. With neither the security of her role in marriage nor the secret retreat of Room Nineteen available to her, she takes the least painful course to banish her personal demons.

RAY BRADBURY

The Golden Apples of the Sun

(p. 698)

In a realm where the vastness of space makes human schemes
of order irrelevant, the captain's unscientific "compass"
direction nonetheless has a certain metaphoric truth to it.
Using an earth-centered standard of judgment, he puts the
quest into a familiar perspective: the journey to the sun
evokes images of travel toward blazing deserts, an especially
appropriate picture for an astronaut in the arctic environment
of this rocket. The need to use the familiar indices the
captain and crew attempt to apply (direction, name of
trajectory, temperature, and time) becomes even more urgent
as the destination makes such attempts at measurement and
judgment close to absurd.

The captain's childhood memory of the last icicle of
winter represents another metaphoric attempt to put the
quest in perspective: the last icicle of a scientific
winter will be melted when the astronauts return with their
handful of sun. On the narrative level, however, this
remembrance of childhood awe is evoked by a melting icicle
within the cabin -- a signal that spurs the captain and
crew back into action. Throughout the story, the shifts
between the narrative and captain's reflections lends the
quest itself greater significance. The captain, we discover,
is no mindless technician simply doing a job, but a thinking,
feeling, human being who questions the nature of this voyage
and is ambivalent about its outcome and motivations.

The myths referred to at the beginning of the story
suggest two possible outcomes: Prometheus is the successful
fire-bringer who has dared the gods, while Icarus's foolish
daring melts the wings that propel him too close to the sun.

120

When the auxiliary refrigeration fails, the <u>Copa de Oro</u> nearly meets the same fate as Icarus, but they will perhaps be hailed as Promethean in their success when they return to Earth. It might be noted that Prometheus was ultimately punished by the gods for his actions; perhaps Bretton's death is a foreshadowing that there will be a price to pay for such daring. The captain's parallel between himself and the primitive man who discovered fire signals his humility and his belief that man is still groping toward civilization in the same primitive manner in spite of his sophisticated technology. Though he is in the atomic age, man's knowledge is still "pitiful and small"; this quest may seem "Promethean," but the captain understands that its significance is not greater than the "primitive" discovery of fire.

The results of the voyage, the captain realizes, will seem like giant strides of advancement, but the motivations behind it are perhaps not merely scientific. The journey to the sun, he concludes, springs from "the pride and vanity of little insect men" as well as their intellectual, material, and religious impulses. The reference to the sun's plasma as "the flesh of God" and the captain's poetic characterization of the sun as a "burning Tree" allude to still another myth: that of the Tree of Knowledge. Taking a piece of the sun thus becomes analogous to the fall from Eden; it is a burning quest of knowledge for its own sake. The quest to the sun may also be seen in non-mythic terms as a metaphor for any intense moment of discovery, which moves from the heat of illumination (south) back toward the coolness of reflection (north).

MAVIS GALLANT

Acceptance of Their Ways

(p. 703)

Gallant was born in Montreal in 1922, but has lived chiefly on the Continent after moving to Paris in 1950. Her fiction, much of which has been published in <u>The New Yorker</u>, reflects her interest in cultural stereotypes and in the conflicts between and within different cultures. In this story, as in many others, she explores the nuances of the thoughts and actions of characters who live on the edge of their social, economic, or cultural circle. Gallant paints a vivid portrait of three ladies who live in an atmosphere of "regularly aired decay." All of them survive on limited incomes yet strive to keep intact some of the manners of the upper class. The contradictions, concessions, and self-deceptions involved in such an endeavor are conveyed not only by their actions but also by the author's restrained irony, humor, and sudden shifts in tone.

We learn a great deal about the process by which Lily became "this curious, two-faced Lily Littel." What we discover isn't very complimentary. She had previously been "a Mrs. Cliff Little, who had taken advantage of the disorders of the war to get rid of Cliff," and later a paid companion who had wished her employer dead. She is ambivalent about Mrs. Freeport and Mrs. Garnett. On the one hand she views them as "ailing, peevish elderly children" who must be humored. Yet she admires the nonchalance with which the two women carry off their affectations of gentility. She notes their bickering, pettiness, and poverty, yet wonders "if there remained a great deal more to learn before she could wear their castoff manners as her own." That Lily accepts this "bleached existence" as superior is implied by her diary entry: "I live with gentlewomen now."

All three women share a capacity for self-deception. Mrs. Garnett is a closet eater. Mrs. Freeport maintains her illusion of gentility and enjoys feeling served even though what she is served is only old cheese "under its coat of pale fur." Lily is a closet drinker who envies the air of "infirm nicety" in the two older women. Lily's attitude and position are delightfully captured in such sentences as: "But she did not take her eyes from Mrs. Freeport, whose blazing eyes perfectly matched the small sapphires hanging from her ears. Lily could have matched the expression if she had cared to, but she hadn't arrived at the sapphires yet."

JAMES BALDWIN

Sonny's Blues

(p. 709)

Although the title of Baldwin's story points to Sonny as the main focus, the narrator's struggle to understand his brother's blues receives equal, if not more, attention. Instead of following chronological time, the narrative begins in the middle, so that we understand the narrator's present condition and then participate with him in exploring the significance of past events. Thus Harlem, Sonny's drug problem, the death of the narrator's daughter, and jazz "become real" to us as the story progresses and the narrator gradually comprehends their full significance. Students might be encouraged to follow this repeated central motif of "becoming real" throughout the story and to use this concept as a means of evaluating the narrator's success in drawing closer to his brother.

The early scene between the narrator and Sonny's aimless friend raises the essential question of responsibility; if this friend feels somewhat responsible for Sonny's plight because he once praised heroin's euphoric effects, then the narrator's neglect becomes an even more significant contribution to Sonny's decline. In addition, this conversation represents the narrator's faltering attempt to bridge the gap between himself and Sonny's world. Although both grew up in the same environment -- Harlem's housing projects -- the narrator seems to have risen above the "darkness" he perceives as its dominant condition. He is sensitive to its claim on his soul, but, even though he still lives there, keeps himself insulated until his brother's plight re-awakens him and forces him to bring the outside world in.

Sonny's struggle, on the other hand, is to get outside of himself. Never talkative, he keeps his own counsel not only because the world around him seems threatening but also because music provides him with his means of expression -- his only way out of the confusion. Initially, the narrator cannot accept Sonny's chosen profession because it falls short of being a practical way to make a living. As he later realizes, however, Sonny is "at that piano playing for his life." After witnessing the religious revival, the narrator notes that music "soothes a poison out"; it is not the cause of Sonny's heroin addiction so much as a possible antidote to it. This incident serves as an essential first step in communication between the brothers; it is the point at which the narrator begins to <u>listen</u> receptively, as he will to Sonny's musical blues at the conclusion.

Without his daughter's death, however, these lines of communication would never have opened. "My trouble made his real," the narrator observes, since it attunes him to the possibility of tragedy striking even the most ordered of lives. In the end, he learns from his brother that he can neither protect Sonny from Harlem's evil or ignore its potential influence. To be his brother's keeper, he must treat him as Creole does onstage. Sonny's blues song becomes a metaphor of his struggles, and conveys to the narrator that "deep water and drowning were not the same thing." Baldwin uses Sonny to illustrate the theme that the artist's suffering may not be unique, but instead of wallowing in it, he creates art that expressively communicates his personal vision of how to endure it. The complementary theme which lends this story its depth, however, is that conveyed by the narrator's new understanding that all men experience their own blues and suffer with others, in a common bond of brotherhood.

WILLIAM GASS

In the Heart of the Heart of the Country

(p. 730)

The narrator's motives for retreating to the heart of the
country are stated almost immediately: he is "in retirement
from love . . . I'm the sort now in the fool's position of
having love left over which I'd like to lose." The place
to which he has physically retreated is a small Indiana
town, but "B," as the opening quotation from Yeats indicates,
is Byzantium, the world of beauty and imagination, the
realm in which he seeks consolation for his romantic
disappointment. What love the narrator has in reserve he
lavishes on his imaginative creations: his poetry and this
story, an impressionistic attempt to come to terms with
loss. The journal form Gass uses is very effective in
conveying the narrator's state of mind. He apprehends the
surrounding world in fragments, reflectively using his
verbal talents to transform and understand his past and
present situations. As he continually returns to the same
topics, the narrator progressively examines the role of his
imagination in his self-restoration.

Students may note that the narrator's attitude toward
"B" (the town) is not consistent, but should be encouraged
to examine why. While he desperately attempts to find
simplicity and beauty, he cannot ignore its spiritual
poverty, social decay, and winter grayness. Although he
attempts to be a sympathetic observer of Mrs. Desmond and
Billy Holsclaw, his keen, ironic consciousness undercuts
this sympathy. Continually referring to himself as part of
the town, the narrator nonetheless does all within his
power to remain separate from it and read all of its
significant features as analogous to his spiritually
alienated condition.

The narrator's formula for recovery involves "living in" -- in other words, retreating into himself and his imagination until he undergoes an emotional healing and rebirth. Through his art, he attempts to hold life at a safe distance and re-connect himself with the outside world (the window in the section "House, My Breath and Window" represents a useful metaphor for his art). Yet, as he comes to understand, he fails at the roots of experience, and his idealizations of "B," nature, and childhood are but "lies of poetry." After living temporarily deep in the heart of himself, the narrator realizes he cannot live only in Byzantium: "Body equals being, and if your weight goes down, you are the less." Self-consciousness of imagination's artifice sends him back to the palpable world, yet the poetic and linguistic constructs he has engaged in have served as more than mere escapism because they bring him in contact with that outside himself. Although the story hardly concludes on a note of triumph, there is a temporary hiatus in the narrator's dialogue with himself, and an uneasy peace with the dry and joyless world awaiting Christmas.

FLANNERY O'CONNOR

Judgement Day

(p. 747)

Although it takes place in New York City, "Judgement Day" is another of O'Connor's stories of the South, its way of life, its racial relations, its religion. Tanner finds that the North is "no kind of place." O'Connor vividly portrays his sense of bewilderment in the unfamiliar world of the big northern city where blacks are actors instead of preachers and lack Tanner's view of the proper relationship between blacks and whites. By telling the story from the point of view of the old man, O'Connor is able to bring us into partial sympathy with Tanner to understand his feelings of confusion and helplessness. He is part of a past whose manners and mores are unsuited to the present world. His death position on the stairway, with his head and arms between the spokes of the bannister and his feet dangling over the stairwell "like those of a man in the stocks," reflects the North's judgement on this old, uneducated, prejudiced Georgia moonshiner.

Tanner is concerned with a different kind of judgement: "The judgement is coming," he tells his daughter, "The sheep'll be separated from the goats . . . Them that did the best they could with what they had from them that didn't." The old man believes that he belongs in the former class. He has no fear of Judgement Day and can imagine nothing worse than the cold, crowded, impersonal world of New York City with its subways, escalators, and elevators. After his first fifteen-minute sightseeing excursion he remains in the apartment. We have an insight into Tanner's character and former way of life as we watch him imagine going through the city with Coleman. We see that for all

his superficial contempt for "niggers," Tanner is much
closer to Coleman than to his daughter or son-in-law. The
way he watches out for Coleman in a critical, protective
manner during his imaginary tour of New York with him tells
us a great deal about Tanner's deep feeling for his friend
of thirty years. The South that Tanner is going home to is
very different from that of his youth -- as is indicated by
the new economic and social power of the black doctor. In
a sense we might conclude that Tanner is going home to
Coleman and the last remnants of a social fabric which has
almost disappeared.

FLANNERY O'CONNOR

Good Country People

(p. 759)

By beginning this tale with an account of Mrs. Hopewell and
Mrs. Freeman, O'Connor establishes a context for Hulga's
contempt for the simple-minded pleasures of good country
people. Her mother's mindless clichés and Mrs. Freeman's
endlessly repetitive conversations concerning her daughter's
gastrointestinal functions are the central social activity on
the farm. Hulga retreats into her philosophical theories
and phrases which are as meaningless to her mother as the
clichés are to Hulga. Despite her disdain for her mother,
Hulga resembles Mrs. Hopewell in her ability to view reality
through a fixed set of formulated phrases and attitudes.
Their reactions to the Bible salesman are surprisingly similar.

When Manley Pointer apologizes for his simplicity and
country ways, Mrs. Hopewell protests that "good country
people are the salt of the earth." Hulga prides herself on
her ability to see beyond such sentimentality. She has no
use for pets, birds, or flowers, and "looked at nice young
men as if she could smell their stupidity." Yet Hulga too
is deceived by Pointer's apparent simplicity. His conversation
during their walk is even more clichéd than Mrs. Hopewell's,
yet Hulga comes to feel that for the first time in her life
she has encountered true innocence. Pointer's comment that
her wooden leg makes her different from everyone strikes
Hulga as possessing metaphysical significance. It was the
first time that anyone "had touched the truth about her."

The ironic reversal of the story stems from Hulga's
haughty confidence that she is one of the few who could
"see through to nothing." Her condescending attitude toward
people and religion keeps her from seeing the artifices of

the traveling salesman. Her atheism, like her feelings of superiority, is an act of will. Faith is not a matter of thought but of belief. By not engaging her intellect, by appearing too simple to be true, the Bible salesman is able to awaken feelings of affection, trust, and faith: "It was like losing her own life and finding it again, miraculously, in his." The true cynic is the salesman who, even as he disappears, continues his stream of clichés. Hulga is left without her protective intellectual shield, literally and figuratively on her knees. She has been deceived but also enlightened. She can now see in the salesman the result of a calculated, solipsistic approach to society and religion.

GABRIEL GARCÍA MÁRQUEZ ≡

A Very Old Man with Enormous Wings

Translated by Gregory Rabassa

The subtitle of this story by Columbian author and Nobel
Prize Winner, Gabriel García Márquez, "A Tale for Children,"
is at once appropriate and ironic. In its use of fantasy
and fanciful humor the story certainly resembles a fairy
tale. However, the satirical presentation of the townsfolk's
responses to the "angel," the uncomfortably surrealist
quality of the fantasy, the many unexplained mysteries
(such as the multitudes of crabs crawling into Pelayo's
house, the strange disease of the pilgrims, and, most
importantly, the nature of the old man with enormous wings),
and the symbolically rather than directly expressed moral,
render this parable too obscure even for many an adult's
liking.

When the winged man is first discovered, he seems
astoundingly strange to Pelayo and readers alike. Yet, in
spite of the poetically satisfying explanation of his
presence given by the know-it-all neighbor (that he was a
weary angel of death sent to fetch the sick child), the
miraculous is soon assimilated to the mundane. Pelayo and
his wife choose to ignore the inexplicable wings, regard
the old man as a castaway sailor, and soon domesticate him
to their imaginations to the extent of treating him like an
overgrown chicken.

The parish priest cannot accept the old man's presumed
celestial origins, as he does not speak Latin and seems far
too human. The priest thus forgets that Christ's humanity
was as much a stumbling block to his contemporaries as it
was essential to the mystery of the divine incarnation.
The old man is Christ-like in his supernatural patience,

although he is more successful as a freakshow than as a healer. The fact that Pelayo and Elisenda so readily put him to commercial use is a sad reflection on the limitations of the ordinary individual's imagination.

The "angel's" popularity is eventually eclipsed by the arrival of the woman who had been changed into a spider for having disobeyed her parents. The attraction this freak has for the townsfolk reflects not only their fickle taste for novelty, but also their preference for a more trite and comprehensible moral than that which the old man presents. His ungainly escape or "resurrection" at the end of the story, watched by Elisenda as she continues with the mundane task of cutting onions, leaves the reader with ambivalent feelings. One understands her relief at the escape of a celestial being who is about as attractive as "a senile vulture," but also feels a sense of loss at the inability of humans to respond appropriately to the strangely miraculous.

URSULA K. LE GUIN

Schrödinger's Cat

(p. 777)

Le Guin has been widely recognized for her fantasy and
science-fiction stories. She won the Nebula award in 1969
for The Left Hand of Darkness and again in 1975 for The
Dispossessed. In 1973 she was awarded the National Book
Award for The Farthest Shore. Although "Schrödinger's Cat"
may be considered a fantasy or science-fiction tale, its
appeal is not limited to readers of that genre. The story
raises a number of intriguing questions concerning the
nature of language, of reality, and of man's quest for
certainty. Her humorous approach allows Le Guin to make
observations on these profound issues without resorting to
elaborate, methodical, dry analyses of various scientific
and philosophical problems.

   Much of the humor of this story comes from the use of
metaphorical expressions in a literal sense. We are not
accustomed to thinking of a person as "coming apart," or as
"a mass of nerves," literally. Furthermore, the narrator
shows no sign that such terms are being used as puns. The
world of the narrator is one in which such terms can be
used literally. It is a world in which a subjective
description is given an objective reality. Besides making
the story interestingly bizarre, such an approach draws our
attention to the way we use language to shape our view of
reality, of particular experiences. To a great extent
language limits and defines reality for us. When the
meanings of words are changed even slightly, or when words
are used in a different context, our sense of reality
becomes disoriented. We have become so comfortable with
the conventions of our language that we are surprised

134

and amused when Le Guin reminds us that such terms as "a real cool cat" or "the poor son of a bitch" could have a literal meaning.

Just as Le Guin pushes the conventions of language to extremes, she also shows us that the "logical" principles of science can appear ridiculous when looked at from another angle. Certainly high heat and rapid molecule movement are related. But the narrator's account that in the extreme heat "worms shot like subway trains through the dirt of gardens, among the writhing roots of roses" reminds us not to carry our theories too far.

This short tale suggest that there is no objective reality, no certainty, outside that which our language and our scientific theories impose on events. Rover -- and humans similar to him -- builds his box to experiment on the cat in order to make certain that everything is uncertain: "To know for <u>sure</u> that God <u>does</u> play dice with the world." But even this degree of certainty is not granted to him. Such a state may be a little scary, but as the narrator remarks early in the tale, "man is most human at his most frightened."

JOHN BARTH

Lost in the Funhouse

(p. 783)

"For whom is the funhouse fun?" Barth asks at the beginning
of the story. Many students may not initially appreciate
the playful spirit of "Lost in the Funhouse"; they may feel
that Barth is merely having fun at the reader's expense.
Barth's commentary on his story and its place in the volume
of the same name sheds some light on his more serious purposes:

> I meant to look back -- at the narrator Ambrose's
> earlier youth, . . . and at some classical manners and
> concerns of the conventional realist-illusionist short
> story -- and also "forward," to some less conventional
> narrative matters and concerns as well as to some
> future, more mythic avatars of the narrator. Finally,
> I meant it to be accessible, entertaining, perhaps
> moving; for I have no use for merely cerebral inventions,
> formalistic tours de force, and place and time --
> tidewater Maryland, World War Twotime -- are pungent
> in my memory.

Embedded in "Lost in the Funhouse" is a story about a
sensitive adolescent and his trip to Ocean City with his
family; complementing this story are reflections on the art
of storytelling related through the consciousness of an
older Ambrose, who is passing through an artistic adolescence
as he constructs his funhouse for his readers. In essence,
Barth's story is a narration about the older Ambrose's
attempt to shape his youthful experience at the shore into
a meaningful and coherent narrative.

Although the "World War Twotime" setting might at first seem merely a device to ground the story in some physical and temporal reality, Barth's attention to the presence of German U-boats and the shortages of commodities signals the importance of funhouses (and fiction) as a diversion or retreat from reality. Both Ambrose and the reader (as well as the narrator) become lost in the funhouse as the story progresses. For Barth, the funhouse serves as a metaphor for fiction itself, and young Ambrose's journey through its twisting paths represents his artistic initiation. The reader too winds his way through a labyrinth as he encounters unfinished sentences (dead ends), the narrator's reflections on the story's course (a hall of mirrors), and the discursive side trips that explain various fictional techniques. The narrator is hardly the secret operator of funhouses he wishes to be, for he parades the principles of its operation in front of the reader while he self-consciously struggles through its construction. Though he continually doubts his success, the result is not a place of "fear and confusion" but rather a journey through his artistic fears and confusions to a discovery of the type of story he must write.

Students might examine whether Barth does indeed utilize some of the fictional strategies he seems to be self-consciously parodying, especially the narrative structures he mentions. Like the narrator of Joyce's "Araby," he discovers new meaning in his past and transmutes it into art, but in a much more modern and self-reflective key. Ambrose the character remains lost in the funhouse, but the older narrator remains outside, simultaneously examining his younger self and his fictional path. "Lost in the Funhouse" may also be profitably compared with Barthelme's "The Balloon," since both stories metaphorically examine the art of fiction as they self-consciously relate what might, in other hands, be material for a more traditional story.

DONALD BARTHELME ≡≡≡≡≡

The Balloon

(p. 798)

Like the authorities in the story who fruitlessly search
the balloon for a point of entry, students lacking familiarity
with modern art may be unable to find a point of entry into
"The Balloon." The recent highly-publicized work of an
artist named Christo, who surrounded a series of islands
with filmy pink plastic, should serve as a good comparison
to the balloon, since both works represent artistic
"statements" which concentrate on aesthetics rather than
meaning. Barthelme provides other comparisons within the
story, such as green and blue paper lanterns and the messages
scrawled on the balloon -- both more purposeful than the
balloon itself.
  The balloon may represent both modern art in general
and modern fiction in particular; given Barthelme's cautions
about the over-insistence on meaning, however, students
might justifiably draw back from any symbolic reading of
"The Balloon." The reactions of the different groups of
people to the balloon provide a clue to the manner in which
Barthelme wishes a reader to react to his story. Daring
children simply jump on and enjoy the balloon, bouncing
and leaping as they cannot on the hard ground. Similarly,
a reader might simply experience modern art in the same
fashion -- for the release it provides from reality. But
Barthelme and the narrator both imply that their balloons
are not merely for amusement. Still, the adults who merely
respond to the balloon as "interesting" or who react with
hostility or mistrust fail to confront the enigma it
presents. Since it possesses a "deliberate lack of finish"
and "was not limited, or defined," the balloon becomes

138

somewhat of a blank slate which others may read in almost
any fashion they wish. The continually changing shape of
the balloon is thus a pleasing diversion from everyday
reality, just as art itself offers an experience "in
contradistinction to the grid of precise, rectangular pathways
under our feet." Since the balloon appears in a bleak
January in Manhattan, the fact that it is interposed between
people and their "sky" should not, the narrator remarks, be
great cause for concern.

Just as the narrative voice controls the story, the
narrator controls the expansion of the balloon. The story's
surprising last paragraph gives this disembodied voice a
sudden reality and reveals a "motive" for the balloon that
should not undercut any of the city dwellers' readings.
For the narrator, the balloon is a "spontaneous autobiographical
disclosure," springing from feelings of loss and sexual
deprivation; like any work of art, the balloon arises from
personal sources which are perhaps disjunct from the viewer's
or reader's experience. The narrator guides us through an
examination of what the balloon is not, what it means to
others, and what it discloses about himself, but leaves
each reader to his own "intersection" with the balloon.

JOHN UPDIKE

A & P

(p. 802)

As in Anderson's "I'm a Fool," the first-person point of
view in "A & P" is essential for establishing the intensely
personal, humorous tone of the story. It allows Sammy to
describe the people and events in the store in his own
idiom and often to reveal more of his character than he
realizes. The slang and seemingly unstructured flow of the
narrative allow us to feel Sammy's enthusiasm and spontaneity.
He is interested in observing and appreciating the girls,
not in glaring at them, as do the women in the aisles. The
informal, enthusiastic language also reflects Sammy's image
of himself as young, sensual, and much more alive than the
adults who surround him. His description of the shoppers
as "sheep" and "houseslaves" indicates his opinion of their
intelligence and lifestyle.

Updike vividly contrasts the casual, carefree world of
Sammy and the three young women with the "respectable" --
or in Sammy's view narrow-minded -- adult world. Lengel's
comment that the girls should be "decently dressed" represents
much more than his personal taste. Sammy notes that the
manager "teaches Sunday School and the rest." "The rest"
implies embracing a lifestyle and ethical code that value
social respectability and propriety over more immediate
impulses such as spontaneity and sensuality. That Lengel
represents traditional, unimaginative values of adult middle
America is underscored by the fact that his store is "right
in the middle of town" near two banks, a church, a newspaper
store, and three real-estate offices.

Sammy instinctively sides with Queenie and her two
companions. His action is impulsive but consistent with his

view of the adult world. To him the girls are more decent than the "witch about fifty with rouge on her cheekbones." The witch gets excited about the mistake at the check-out counter, Lengel gets excited about the casual flouting of company policy, but neither of them sees what Sammy and Stokesie see: the romance of Queenie gliding momentarily through the drab commercial aisles of the A & P. Sammy's flippant descriptions and comments should not keep students from perceiving that he makes several astute remarks on social norms: "Policy is what the kingpins want. What the others want is juvenile delinquency." That Sammy is not a rebel in search of a cause but, on the contrary, a rather easy-going young man makes his decision to quit more significant. Although it is in protest to conventional adult values, Sammy's decision to quit -- and his realization that it is "fatal" not to go through with it -- marks an important step in his maturation. The world will be a harder place for him because it will force him to make decisions, often between his security and his sense of fairness, and to live with his choices.

JOYCE CAROL OATES

The Going-Away Party

(p. 807)

"The Going-Away Party" presents an episode in which a
seemingly controlled and secure future begins to recede
from the protagonist's grasp. Marya Knauer, the proud,
self-confident valedictorian of her high school class,
appears to be destined for a successful career at the State
University, yet her attraction to Emmett Schroeder complicates
her plans. Discussion of Marya's character might profitably
focus on the amount of sympathy which we feel for her and
on the effect of the information offered parenthetically by
the narrator on our sympathies. Marya's disdainful
superiority, her insularity, and her overriding need to be
in control in social interactions are hardly endearing
qualities, but behind them we discover her genuine desires
to be part of her peer group and to be loved, both of which
are subverted by her vigilant self-awareness.

While Marya wants nothing more than to leave Innisfail
and "begin again, give birth to herself," she has linked
her self-image to Emmett, to whom she is drawn by his sense
of superiority and her undeniable sexual desires. Emmett
presents a challenge to Marya, but instead of becoming her
coveted prize, he turns into a subtle tormentor who knows
her nature better than she does. Mildly sadistic, Emmett
comes across at times as an almost sinister character, yet
his relationship with Marya simply disintegrates rather
than erupting into violence. Curiously, Emmett drops out of the
story just before its cruel and violent climax. Oates thus
makes it difficult for us to explain the brutality as a
simple result of Emmett's villainy and forces us to re-
examine Marya's role in the affair.

Despite her valedictory speech on the "'repellent' nature of American conformity," Marya eagerly accepts the invitation to the going-away party as a final opportunity to affirm that her peers are her friends. As Marya drinks, the events become less clearly focused in her mind, and the shift in verb tense and style in this final scene lends the climax a more immediate impact. She becomes the victim of senseless and drunken violence which robs her of her mark of distinction: her long hair, to which Oates devotes brief attention at key points within the story. "It was hers but it wasn't her," Marya reflects about her hair; like her sarcasm and wit, she uses her hair for effect. Nonetheless, she is symbolically shorn of part of her identity when the boys clip it off. Spencer's "The Girl Who Loved Horses" might be treated in conjunction with this story, since both deal with women whose sense of control diminishes when they encounter some kindred spirit.

TONI CADE BAMBARA

Raymond's Run

(p. 821)

According to Mary Helen Washington, the focus of Toni Cade Bambara's writing is often on "black women at the edge of a new awareness . . . who create their own choices about the women they want to be." The narrator of "Raymond's Run," the streetwise Squeaky, is certainly such a character. The effectiveness of the story depends largely on the unusually toughminded and unsentimental perspective that an underprivileged childhood on New York's West Side has afforded this little girl. She is nevertheless admirable in her fierce defensiveness towards her retarded brother, Raymond, and in the fact that she makes no bones about trying hard to succeed in life. In the latter she acts in sharp contrast to the more privileged girl, Cynthia, who pretends that her achievements come easily.

The fact that the narrator is a girl allows Bambara to explore and criticize the ways in which girls are socialized to behave. The athletic Squeaky sees the absurdity in her mother's wanting her to dress up in feminine clothes they can't afford and in "trying to act like a fairy or a flower" or even, more ludicrously, a strawberry in a Hansel and Gretel pageant. It could be argued that the author sometimes ascribes insights to her narrator that are perhaps beyond such a young girl, as when she spells out the maxim, "you should be trying to be yourself, whatever that is" or when she says (in response to the hypocritical smiles of the rival gang) "I'm thinking that girls never really smile at each other because they don't know how and there's probably no-one to teach us how, cause grownup girls don't know either." As the above mentioned critic has said, "the

trouble with deliberately creating models is that they slip
all too easily out of character . . . into being mouthpieces
for the author's ideology."

The May Day race does bring Squeaky to a new awareness.
Though glad to have won, she senses a new feeling of pride
in her brother's achievement that makes her consider, for
the first time, the possibility of helping someone else be
the star. This should not be seen as a return to the set
definitions of sexual roles, but rather as a new generosity
of spirit which allows her to smile, genuinely, at her
rival, with a feeling of respect for the latter's
"professionalism." The story thus suggests a new basis on
which more satisfying relations between people, and women
in particular, can be built.

PART II

Gift of Grass

(p. 835)

Probing for a single reason for Cathy's final gesture is perhaps antithetical to the spirit of the ending, in which Bill's rationality dissolves "like clouds or shadows" and gives way to emotion. Cathy's gift is motivated neither by simple pity nor by a perception that Bill is "hip" enough to try marijuana. Instead, it springs from a recognition of Bill's essential humanity; thus, the gift of grass is essentially an act of communication across the gulf that divides youth and middle age.

With Dr. Fredericks, on the other hand, Cathy has difficulty communicating. Adams sketches him as an obtuse representative of the status quo who is more interested in promoting "normalcy" than in assisting his young patient in her search for her identity. Barbara and Bill have previously turned to Fredericks to patch their marriage, yet Bill's decision not to leave was made before they even entered the psychiatrist's office. Ironically, Fredericks is a better financial counselor than an emotional one, and it is his investment advice rather than his therapy sessions which helps the marriage become more stable.

At home, in the living room, no one seems to sit in his or her implicitly designated piece of furniture; Barbara, in designing the room, has attempted to impose certain roles into which neither Bill nor Cathy neatly fits. Faced with Bill's infidelity, Barbara's perfectionism, the strain of middle age, and problems with Cathy, the parents conduct a ritual "cocktail hour" as a release. Cathy uses marijuana for "the melting of her despair"; despite her giggling, she appears to be more tranquil in her escape than her parents are in theirs. Yet both drugs are not causes but symptoms of some larger problem which the family must solve.

Bill and Cathy tentatively begin an approach to easing the immediate family tensions in the final scene, when they discover their common dislike of Fredericks, hatred of deer-hunters, and discomfort with themselves as they are. Though their communication may be indirect, its success is measured by Cathy's gesture. Bill's tears and peaceful, unthinking sleep at the story's conclusion parallel the epiphany in the park which Cathy experiences after visiting Fredericks. Both represent temporary releases from their confusions and retreats from their everyday roles which might enable them to face their problems more clearly.

MARGARET ATWOOD

The Man from Mars

(p. 841)

"The Man from Mars," as the title indicates, is a story
about an "alien" -- one who at first seems harmless and
confused but gradually becomes a more threatening outsider.
Both Christine and her mother pride themselves on their
tolerance of foreigners, but their complacent liberality of
feeling is put to the test by Christine's persistent admirer.
The story's opening reveals the special veneration Christine
reserves for foreigners: while she draws back from the old
men with "wrinkled toadstool faces" and refuses to feed the
"ratlike" squirrels, she consistently attempts to be pleasant
to the foreigner and to construe his motives charitably. She
is involved with the United Nations Club and takes the
unpopular Arab role in the Mock Assembly, but has not
confronted the reality of what it means to be "a person
from another culture." Similarly, her mother's practice of
hiring foreign girls as servants represents a token gesture
rather than a true attempt to bridge cultures.

Initially, Christine humors her "friend" and feels she
is doing her "bit for internationalism," but her continued
tolerance creates a situation that spirals out of her
control as she becomes the pursued. After her friend uses her
as prop in his souvenir photograph, she feels violated but
manages to laugh off his pathetic attempt to capture her.
Yet the foreigner captures more than her photographic image
by continually insinuating himself on her consciousness;
his pursuit creates a mystique about Christine in which she
revels until she learns about her friend's similar stalking
of a sixty-year-old Mother Superior. Her inflated self-
image is thus punctured, but the mystery of his motivations

enables her to put the incident behind her and steer her life back onto its appointed course.

Although the foreigner might seem a stereotypical "inscrutable Oriental," alert students might use the clues Atwood provides (his French accent and the "odd assemblage of Gs, Ys, and Ns" in his name) to establish his nationality: Vietnamese. Students who want to read Atwood's story as an allegory of U.S. involvement in Vietnam should be reminded that the story takes place in Canada and should be steered back to the main theme of clashing cultures. Because Christine's friend reveals very little about himself, the story takes on some elements of the absurd. Like Christine, we are unsure of his motivation and unable to ascribe any logical cause-and-effect pattern to the events. Finally, however, Christine reaches some understanding of her friend when she transcends her fear and senses her true kinship with him in the last lines of the story.

ANN BEATTIE

A Clever-Kids Story

(p. 854)

"A Clever-Kids Story" examines the tension between the problematic adult world, represented by Jane's parents and Sebastian, and the idealized realm of childhood on which it impinges. Joseph's "clever-kids" stories embody the essence of childhood freedom and pure escapism. Within these stories, Joseph is able to exercise absolute control within a fantasy world where the clever kids (he and his sister) prevail. The change in Joseph's stories from fantastic accounts of cleverness to trite fabrications of personal heroics marks the separation of the clever kids and the dangers of a retreat into illusion. Whether or not Joseph believes in his own invulnerability, he is neither unconventional enough to flee to Canada and avoid the draft nor clever enough to evade death in Vietnam.

Jane's first-person narrative adopts the same title as her brother's narratives, thus inviting comparison between the two varieties of storytelling. Unlike Joseph's stories, which are straightforward narratives with miraculous resolutions, Jane's piecemeal story is related by an emotionally-numbed consciousness still attempting to come to terms with loss. Her story incorporates rather than evades the problems of adulthood she has witnessed: death, abortion, divorce, and nervous breakdowns. An ironic stance is one defense against such complexities -- one which Jane adopts temporarily but attempts to move beyond. As she re-examines her childhood, she wonders whether she was naively unconscious of the adult world's pervasive irony, which she now perceives in Joseph's refusal to escape to Canada, the letter from his friend, and the birth of her father's child.

Unlike Sebastian, her parents' faithful friend, Jane refuses to let Joseph's death and the disintegration of her family kill her spirits. With Nick she attempts to find happiness, even though she is pulled back into the past by her enduring connections with her family and her memories of Joseph. Her family maintains its bond in shared sorrow, yet each wants to remember Joseph differently. At one point, Jane fondly remembers that his method of waking her up "was nicer than any kiss," the manner in which Nick awakens her. Joseph remains the idealized clever kid whose powers she wishes she could reassume to banish the demons of adulthood and tragedy. In the final scene in Joseph's old bedroom, Jane attempts to play the role her brother once filled before the two children were assigned separate bedrooms. When she crawls into bed with Nick, he becomes the half-asleep auditor of her fantasy about "demons." Instead of telling a clever-kids story, however, Jane acquiesces to his sexual overtures, "not knowing what to say." The world of childhood, she realizes, cannot be recaptured so easily; the demons cannot be totally banished by either imaginative play or her present love -- only held at bay.

CLARK BLAISE

A Class of New Canadians

Unlike the foreign students to whom he teaches English,
Norman Dyer is a new Canadian who wholeheartedly embraces
his adopted country. Montreal seems to sparkle with all
the "class" that Norman believes the United States lacks;
Norman self-consciously attempts to avoid any examples of
simple bad taste and immerse himself in the classier aspects
of Canadian culture. Yet, in his complacent expatriation,
he ignores Montreal's status as a melting pot, preferring
instead to enjoy the variety of ethnic restaurants that
perhaps should signal this fact to him.

Teaching English as a second language at McGill, Dyer
carries his condescending air of superiority to an extreme.
He feels god-like when he presides over his class of new
Canadians, who do not share his love of everything Canadian.
The members of his English class represent a wider socio-
economic class: expatriates who use Canada as a stopping-
off point on their way to the United States because they
can get by there with their native language until they
learn English. Norman's illusion of self-importance is
undercut when he learns that these foreigners think of
Montreal as merely a place to land and that he plays a role
in the "superstructure of exploitation" that he had hoped
to escape.

Norman reads the passages from Faulkner to illustrate
his superiority and show his students how far they still
have to go. Perhaps meant to illustrate the elasticity of
the language, these passages ironically comment on Norman
himself -- a citadel of Canadian rectitude who is not above
passive vindictiveness in his decision not to correct

Mayor's unidiomatic job application letter. By letting Mayor's errors stand, Dyer attempts to undercut the Spaniard's chances for emigration; he justifies his action as a corrective one that will give Mayor time to earn the clothes he wears -- the very clothes that are withheld from Dyer as the final mark of assimilation. Yet if the clothes in the window could speak, they might indict Dyer for the same "touching vanity and confidence" he perceives in the Spaniard. Like his students, Norman finally tries too hard to forsake one national identity and assume another.

PAUL BOWLES

A Distant Episode

(p. 871)

Joyce Carol Oates's full commentary on this story in the
preface should enable students to grasp the meaning and
understand the technique of Bowles's cautionary tale. As
Gore Vidal notes in his introduction to Bowles's Collected
Stories, "A Distant Episode" is "emblematic of the helplessness of an over-civilized sensibility [the Professor's] when
confronted with an alien culture." Although the Professor,
in his naiveté and arrogance, is somewhat culpable for his
predicament, the senseless violence with which he is punished
seems out of proportion to his "crime." The dispassionate
narrator does nothing to awaken our sympathies for the
Professor, whose unexamined and irrational actions in an
unfamiliar land create a situation in which his helplessness
and inadequacy are magnified.

As he travels to Aïn Tadouirt, he repeats the name of
his friend, the café-keeper, like a protective invocation;
later, before his descent of the cliff, these same words
possess "sinister overtones." The Professor is a linguist
who has come to study dialect variations, but among the
Reguibat he not only loses his capacity for speech but also
fails to decipher their language. He initially attempts to
lessen the horror and absurdity of what happens to him by
assigning words such as "operation" to the cutting out of
his tongue and "predicament" or "situation" to the fear that
grips him in the desert. Yet his descent from the plateau
of academic study into the harsh reality of the desert
nomads renders such linguistic constructs useless, and he
retreats into a wordless world. Though he appears to accept
his fate as a grotesque amusement for nomads, the Professor's

156

emergence from his resignation occurs when he once again feels pain and begins to grope consciously for the meaning of the words he hears and sees. The words on the calendar signal the passage of time and the cruel tricks of fate; after "feeling that he was performing what had been written for him long ago," the Professor breaks from captivity and flees insensibly into the desert.

The irony and foreshadowing present in the story reveal that the events and the environment provided warnings which the Professor might have heeded. His sense of isolation in the village, the qaouaji's uncertainty about tomorrow, the smell of rotten meat, the bothersome dog, and the ruined marabout should indicate the threatening nature of his irrational quest for camel-udder boxes. Yet his "intelligence" convinces him that "it was not so important to probe for explanations" and he foresees that the experience might be a warning -- one which the narrator characterizes as "half sinister, half farcical." The reader recognizes this dual nature of the Professor's experience before he does, though, like the Professor, he may be unprepared for the shocking violence in the unfamiliar desert beneath the lunar chill.

RICHARD BRAUTIGAN ═══════

Revenge of the Lawn
A Short History of Religion
in California

(p. 880)
(p. 884)

Brautigan's ancedotal "Revenge of the Lawn" might be
profitably compared to such early examples of the short
story as Irving's "The Legend of Sleepy Hollow" and Twain's
"The Notorious Jumping Frog of Calaveras County." All
share a concern with legend and a comic tone, but Brautigan's
story seems to be consciously attempting to present a
fragmented history instead of a meticulously crafted story.
Judged by Poe's dictum of the single effect, "Revenge of
the Lawn" would not fare well, as the numerous anecdotes
that the narrator spins shift, rather than concentrate, the
reader's attention. The most obvious relation between
events is their connection with the narrator's past, though
the events he narrates occur well before his earliest
memory. Though the narrator explores the "stormy American
past," he seems unmotivated to assemble it into a coherent
scheme that explains the present. Instead, his family
history is presented as a comedy of errors starring his
grandmother, a successful moonshiner who plucks all the
feathers off the intoxicated geese she believes to be
dead; his grandfather, a "minor Washington mystic" who
thinks he derives his powers from his lawn and who bears
some resemblance to the narrator; and Jack, a one-time
estate con artist who takes the grandfather's place after
the latter is committed for senility and who becomes the
object of the lawn's revenge.

"A Short History of Religion in California," perhaps
less of a "history" than the previous story, is more tightly
constructed and accessible, with a narrator much closer to
the events he relates. His daughter participates in two

religious experiences, one spontaneously occuring in the
natural world, the other organized by a church group. She
is fascinated by the three deer which compose a natural
trinity whose separate gazes may be blended into one, and
prefers them to the cake and the song about the three wise men.
Although the story's title invites speculation about possible
allegorical meaning, to load layers of meaning on Brautigan's
fiction may destroy its understated effect. With her
intuition and uncorrupted sense of awe, the child senses
that nature is inherently more "religious" than organized
religion. In his joy over his daughter's intuitively
"correct" choice, the narrator experiences a momentary
epiphany in which he too communes with nature in restored
faith in human goodness, Brautigan's story may be a parable
of the rediscovery of the vitality and sacredness of nature
in California, but the personal history rather than the
allegory creates the story's thematic effect.

HORTENSE CALISHER

The Scream on Fifty-Seventh Street

(p. 886)

The "apocalypse" of Calisher's story is not the mysterious
scream which obsesses the narrator but rather the discovery
which she makes about herself and her aloneness in the
final pages of the story. As in a traditional detective
story, the protagonist, Mrs. Hazlitt, attempts to assemble
evidence, determine motivation, and locate the "perpetrator."
Yet solving the mystery of the scream does not yield any
evidence of its source; Mrs. Hazlitt is merely concerned
with establishing that the scream was not a product of her
overactive imagination. Ironically, her fears that the
scream has arisen from her own anxiety and loneliness become
prophetic. The cathartic scream which wells in her breast
at the story's conclusion is no longer a mystery because
her "detective work" has led to self-discovery. The identity
of the screamer thus becomes insignificant as long as Mrs.
Hazlitt recognizes that he or she shares her plight.

Recently widowed, Mrs. Hazlitt has returned to the
city in an attempt to learn to live alone because she
believes that the city naturally promotes such fragmentation.
Although she revels in the city's beauties and attempts to
convince herself that she enjoys its advantages, she seems
to long for the country, with its lack of barriers, its
neighborliness, and its memories of her dead husband. She
attempts to dismiss the community she has left as full of
"ready 'casserole' pity," but cannot find any antidote to
the "dark, anarchic version of the city." Her strategies
for deriving comfort in the city are few and are doled out
sparingly lest she begin obsessive behavior.

160

Yet after she hears the scream, Mrs. Hazlitt begins to lose her tight grip on things. Drawn to the scream because she senses it to be some type of signal, she attempts to confirm first its reality and later its "accent." The note of "terror controlled" she senses in it echoes the restraints she places on herself in her widowhood. Mrs. Hazlitt crosses the line of what she has determined to be "acceptable" behavior for a person who is alone when she unburdens herself by addressing the empty chair. While such an action might seem the first step toward insanity, the release it provides is an essential step in overcoming the obsession she has developed. Mrs. Hazlitt ultimately realizes that she is not lonely; she is simply alone. Yet the scream, she learns, represents the invisible community of those who are alone, those who "are still responsible" and refuse to collapse into lonely isolation. In the end, she waits to join this company, not as a madwoman having a fit, but as a fellow sufferer who will confirm to another that he or she is not alone.

BARRY CALLAGHAN ≡≡≡≡≡

The Black Queen

(p. 902)

Because Callaghan employs a number of sterotypical qualities
associated with male homosexuals to characterize Hughes and
McCrae, students may tend to snicker or view the story as a
satire. Detailed examination of these qualities, however,
should generate discussion about the basis and fairness of
such stereotypes, and also bring out the distinguishing
features of the main characters. Close attention to the
story's opening, to the personal conflict, and to the
symbolic significance of the black queen should help modify
simplistic initial reactions and promote a greater
understanding of the issues of security and change which
"The Black Queen" addresses.

On one level, of course, the story depicts a lover's
quarrel, but as the context should make clear, Hughes and
McCrae embody a basic conservatism. Somewhat uncomfortable
with their relationship, they maintain separate bedrooms
and draw back from intimacy; at the same time, they seek
tenderness, dignity, and stability. Like their colonial
house, which stands as a monument to the past in a changing
neighborhood, the men embody traditional values as they
attempt to establish a partnership. They perhaps delude
themselves in believing that they can hold "a perfectly
preserved piece of the past, unsullied, as if everything
didn't have to change, didn't have to end up swamped by
decline and decay." We see their relationship at a static
and troubled stage, beset with subtle social and personal
pressures that threaten their security.

Their collection of rare old stamps represents a
retreat from the present through a collection of mementos

of the stable past. The stamp picturing Queen Victoria in her widow's weeds is particularly appropriate to their collection because it symbolizes the stability of Britain during Victoria's long reign and the ensuing decline of the British empire. Students will easily identify the stamp with the two men because of Callaghan's word play, but may miss its symbolic implications. As a focal point of the men's troubles, it stands as a portent of the eventual decline of their tenuous stability. Significantly, the black queen is also a dead-letter stamp which never reaches its destination.

Ironically, McCrae uses the black queen to send his message of dissatisfaction to Hughes. In forsaking the characteristic Cuban heels which his friend singles out as "affected" and in ruining the valuable stamp, he acts out the potential results of Hughes' discontent. McCrae does more through his gesture than simply display his pique concerning the satirical remarks Hughes makes about his boots and mannerisms; he signals the end of a stable but stagnant relationship -- the inevitable results of change.

Cathedral

(p. 905)

"Cathedral" brings new life to the truism that the blind actually know the surrounding reality better than the sighted. Some background on blind prophets such as Tiresias might be helpful in illustrating Carver's translation of such conventions into a contemporary setting. The narrator, however, is hardly in quest of a seer; he establishes himself as a man of simple tastes and strong opinions. Students should note how he subtly attempts to shape the reader's views and paint a favorable picture of himself; an examination of his biases should enable them to see beyond his opinions and understand his character better than he seems to understand himself.

With blunt and engaging honesty, he remarks that his ideas about blindness come from the movies, reveals that he is no fan of poetry, and dismisses things that do not meet his approval as "pathetic" or "creepy." He and his wife (who exhibits more sensitivity than the narrator) lead a comfortable but relatively unfulfilled existence that depends heavily on television and alcohol to relieve the boredom. Into his life intrudes Robert, the wife's blind friend, first through his tapes and then in person. The narrator's jealousy over his wife's friendship with the blind man intensifies his uneasiness about the latter's supposed handicap. Although the narrator initially feels superior to Robert (he jokes that he will take him bowling, for example), he soon perceives that the blind man will force him to examine his preconceptions and force him to "see" the world in a new light.

Carver introduces the cathedral, a symbol of transcendent spiritual experience, in a natural manner: over the television, the only channel through which it might realistically enter the narrator's life. Although a cathedral initially means nothing in particular to him, it becomes an appropriate vehicle for his revelation. Spiritually blind but able to see, the narrator attempts to communicate his limited concept of a cathedral (its physical structure, its history) to the blind man, who in turn shows him its true essence. Carver's story is a lesson in the blindness of our everyday perceptions and the inadequacy of language for communicating about the surrounding world. When the narrator feels he is not "inside anything," his perception of the cathedral is complete; he has experienced the uplift of the soul that a cathedral attempts to create. By keeping his eyes closed, he escapes from his mundane life in a momentary awareness of the spiritual essence of reality.

Redemption

(p. 915)

The story's title should provide a starting point for
discussion, as it introduces Gardner's dominant moral
question. The strong religious orientation of the upstate
farmers should also provide a clue to the story's theological
dimension. Gardner's story seems to ask whether redemption
is an absolute state that man can achieve or a higher
condition toward which he can only continue to strive.
Neither of the main characters who suffer acutely seems
initially to be headed toward redemption. Dale Hawthorne's
response to his son's death is that of the brooding,
melancholy Romantic; students should note that the mention
of Shelley and Byron is not superfluous. The community
seems to find Dale's womanizing to be a justified retreat
from his grief, but the entire Hawthorne family suffers
further as a result of Dale's actions. Jack's self-imposed
penance is portrayed as the more heroic response; instead
of seeking escape from grief, Jack plunges deeper into
despair and attempts to conquer it while maintaining his
daily responsibilities on the farm. He accepts the increased
burden of work created by his father's periodic absences,
but fails to lose himself in his work. Acutely self-conscious
of his attempts to escape grief, Jack becomes unable to
derive comfort from fantasy or nature; hard work punctuated
by moments of debilitating guilt seems to be his fate until
he takes up the French horn.

    Although the horn receives mention near the beginning
of the story as one of the more "permanent" comforts Jack's
mother has given him, it is prominent only in the last
section. Students might feel that this shift in attention is

contrived, but it might be pointed out that Jack's musical dedication begins after his father's permanent return, when the burden of running the farm has been lifted. Dale's repentance should ring somewhat hollow; the titles of his poems -- "Tomorrow's Bridge" and "This Too Will Pass" -- indicate the cliched sentiments he has embraced. Yegudkin too has been the victim of tragedy, but he manages to preserve the inner fire which Dale seems to have burnt out in his travels. Yegudkin's response to his near death in Siberia is to transcend his misfortune through dedication to art. His consummate skill is evident when he tests the student's new horn, sounding the depths and heights of its expressive possibilities. As Jack's teacher, Yegudkin perhaps represents a father figure for him; at least, he displays how his dedication to art may be a more viable path toward redemption than Dale's pious poetry. Jack realizes that he will never play like Yegudkin, but despite this vision of what skills are beyond his reach, he perceives that such continued dedication is perhaps part of his redemption.

GAIL GODWIN

Dream Children

(p. 924)

No mere argument for the plausibility of psychic phenomena,
"Dream Children" has more far-reaching purposes than students
might at first discern. Godwin's story seeks to challenge
our ordinary conception of "reality" -- a term which its
penultimate paragraph suggests is an extremely relative
one. Mr. McNair is unaware of his wife's double life, and
does not understand her interest in the supernatural. He
draws a strong distinction between daily life and fantasy,
and favors confronting "things as they are" over escapism
and dreaming. His statement not only reveals his imaginative
limitations but also seems an odd one for someone who
produces television comedies. The English scientist and
the nurse who mistakenly hands Mrs. McNair an infant both
undergo experiences that expand their conceptions of reality.
The scientist nicely capsulizes the story's theme with his
argument that dreams and waking life are not competitors
but reciprocal sources of consciousness; the nurse, in her
brief epiphany, recognizes that her accepted reality is
mutable rather than absolute.

Television provides Godwin with an extended analogy
through which we may understand the dream realm, yet its
programs hardly become the stuff of dreams. The transmission
of television programs is scientifically-explained "magic"
which resembles the out-of-body projections of Mrs. McNair
and the child. Yet the ghosts on the screen are retouched
images acting out a script; their connection to real people
seems less substantial than that of the "dream child" in the
McNair house. Victoria Darrow's image will be erased from
the television screen when she is fired from the news program;

as long as Mrs. McNair and the child are in touch with their dream realm, their out-of-body experiences will continue. Their simple existence in and acceptance of the dream realm stands in stark contrast to the pompous self-consciousness exhibited in Mr. McNair's television special.

Godwin's well-crafted story makes use of delayed revelation, which creates an abundance of foreshadowing. Bits of psychic phenomena, Victoria's desire to have a child before she is forty, the mention of a story almost "too incredible for television," and Mrs. McNair's childhood night journey all appear before the stories to which they are connected receive full development, giving the story something of a dream-like texture. The title suggests that Mrs. McNair, herself once a dreamy child until "cured" by the psychiatrist, rejoins the realm of the "Dream Children" with their "magically sagacious powers" when she resumes her night journeys.

WILLIAM GOYEN

Bridge of Music, River of Sand

(p. 933)

"Bridge of Music, River of Sand" presents us with a haunting
and enigmatic image, using a narrative voice that is
compelling in its immediacy. Goyen himself confesses, "I
haven't a clue as to what the story means. It is surely
about loss (in spirit). Yet despite loss, mystery and
beauty remain." The dried-up Trinity River is the most
obvious symbol of diminishment, one which creates a "feeling
of something missing" in the narrator, who is engaged in a
"sentimental trip through home regions." The old bridge
likewise reveals erosion by time and human neglect. Though
it no longer serves its original purpose, the bridge retains
its beauty and serves as the narrator's bridge between the
present and the past. Despite the strains of music his
crossing evokes, the bridge provides no simple passage to a
secure haven of memory. One might interpret the narrator's
crossing as a journey across the River Styx, which
inexplicably claims the life of the naked diver. The
narrator may cross the river, but he is inexorably drawn to
the image of desperation and loss he has witnessed.
     Perhaps one of the reasons augmenting the narrator's
disturbance is his recognition of the leaper as a kindred
spirit -- one who plunges headfirst into life's mysteries.
Both the narrator and the leaper are perhaps searching, in
different ways, for the answer to the question of where the
river has vanished. In his search for explanations, the
narrator wonders whether he may be suffering a form of
"bridge madness" and experiencing some form of delusion.
Yet both his matter-of-fact tone and his incredulity lend
the incident a plausibility that it might not otherwise possess.

170

The horrible image of loss he has witnessed paradoxically creates a compulsive need to affirm that a man <u>was</u> completely consumed by the earth. By giving up his secret to his listeners, he not only searches once more for an explanation but also keeps the leaper from vanishing into nothingness by implanting the image in our memory. The story itself might be equated with the bridge of music; just as the narrator's journey across the bridge evokes forgotten or dormant music, so the story evokes an "odd truth" from an incident that for the narrator has been "lost to fact."

The episode about the narrator's parents is far from a tangential reflection. It not only establishes the narrator's past connection with the bridge but also reveals that others have found the journey across it to be disturbing. Students may be eager to equate the father's jump to save the narrator's mother with the leap recently witnessed, but the former incident is by no means the "source" of his present vision. This memory is the only bit of the past which the narrator recaptures. The story concludes with his descent into the reality of a polluted world covered with a fine mist of Fuller's Earth, a world which perhaps "explains" in its own way the figure's mysterious leap from the bridge.

JOHN HAWKES

Two Shoes for One Foot

(p. 937)

Students (and teachers) will be legitimately baffled about
the particular motivations and incidents of this story,
which Joyce Carol Oates calls "a riddle in itself, not easily
to be answered." Nonetheless, students should recognize
the boys' attempts to cross the threshold into manhood
through their controlled struggle with the Kommandant. The
smallest boys' outbursts signal the nervousness shared by
the whole group, but Heinrich, their leader, restores order
and wages a subtle war of wills with the Kommandant, who
occupies a position of power and embodies their fear of the
unknown.

Neither the Kommandant nor the boys are "complete"
men. The former lacks not only a leg but also any spark of
human compassion; the boys engage in a deadly game to gain
the manhood they crave. We suspect that the boys have
murdered Herr Herzenbrecher, the only complete man in the
story, in order to impress the Kommandant, whose exact
interest in the body never becomes clear. In their "exchange
of heart for heart," the boys become more like the cold-
hearted adult whose depraved purpose is served by this
callous murder. When the smallest boy shouts the title
phrase, he openly taunts the Kommandant in a way that
reveals his own bravery and highlights the absurdity of the
situation. The boys appear to get the better of the
Kommandant, but in their exchange they succumb to the very
evil they seem to fear in him.

Students should study how the story's dramatic tension
is intensified by the setting. The tree branch, following
"some urge dictated by its sap and fibers," scratches on

the window and breaks into Heinrich's childhood room just
as he is about to shatter the barrier that separates him
from adulthood. The growing darkness indicates the boy's
descent into the Kommandant's evil, and the rain which does
not "help the apple trees to grow," signals neither relief
nor growth. Most significant of all, perhaps, is the German
setting and the atmosphere of oppression which pervades the
story.

JOSEPHINE JACOBSEN ====

The Mango Community

(p. 942)

The bureaucratic Vice-Consul's early, matter-of-fact caution
to Jane -- "You're really very isolated here" -- unfortunately
foreshadows the discovery she must make about the island
community in which each member of her small family group
attempts to find a place. Dan's friendship with Alexis
leads to a smooth assimilation into the community, and Dan,
with his dark tan, begins to resemble his native friend.
The instant communion of childhood cuts across the cultural
schism that is evident in Mr. Montrose's distrust of
outsiders. Harry too finds what seems to be a kindred
community in the island's growing passive resistance
movement. Jane's attempts to establish a personal connection
with the community by striking up a friendship with Mrs.
Montrose prove ineffectual because of the cultural distance
between them. Her engagement with the island is that of an
artist with her material. She can sense the beauty and
power of Alexis, for example, but realizes she will never
be close to him in the way that her son is. Her gift of
the mango to the old man represents another attempt to
become part of this mango community, but their lives touch
in only a brief and limited fashion as a result of this
gesture.

For Jane, the island becomes a "mad palette" of color;
the tropical mosaic of color she sees is nicely rendered in
the impressionistic word-paintings Jacobsen presents.
Harry views the island as a stimulus for action, not as
art; as a writer, his medium is that of words, which he
uses in his activism to persuade others and create change.
Jane's painting, on the other hand, seeks to interpret.

She sees her medium as superior to Harry's: her paintings, she believes, are not limited by the quest to create meaning and exhort others to action. In her "cooler" medium she constantly seeks peaceful scenes, while Harry is drawn toward conflict. Harry, despite his attempts to immerse himself in the island's politics, remains a relative outsider, while Jane perhaps manages to move closer to its mystery. Though she draws back from its confusing "evasion of greens" by painting the snowflakes, that painting creates another momentary triumph over cultural barriers when she comprehends Mrs. Montrose's angle of vision.

Alexis's injury creates a temporary split in the family group that the three outsiders have established and also upsets their individual connections with its various communities. At the end of the story, Jane and Harry attempt to establish some peaceful resolution to the situation, but what appears to be the only solution represents merely a temporary armistice among them. "The Mango Community" should raise ethical questions about the individual's responsibility for his actions and his relationship with the various social "communities" -- ranging from family to culture -- to which he belongs.

ALISTAIR MACLEOD

In the Fall

(p. 955)

On the surface, "In the Fall" may seem to be a simple story
about a man's attachment to his horse, but on closer
examination it should produce sensitive reflection on the
themes of change and stability. Though James, the young
narrator, ostensibly relates the story of his parents'
marital tensions, the story concerns himself as much as it
does them. Their conflict of wills transcends the issue of
the horse; in reality, they struggle for power over each
other, though the story's conclusion portrays their
realization that love, not power, will guide them in their
changes. James might be profitably compared with the
narrator of Joyce's "Araby," who also relates a problematic
past experience in order to come to terms with it. James's
vocabulary and use of figurative language reveal that he is
no longer a child when he tells the story. His flat, even
tone indicates that he is attempting to distance himself
emotionally and examine his initiation into adulthood
objectively.

The father's attachment to Scott serves as a substitute
for the relationship with his family that he has lost by
casting himself in the role of provider. Scott's unthinking
animal service promotes an alliance between them that
endures beyond the work season -- an alliance which the
mother seeks to destroy in her quest for security. Frustrated
by her traditional role and her husband's absence, she
holds a more utilitarian view of animals: she raises capons
for sale. These castrated roosters, along with the reined
Ayshire bull, provide appropriate analogies for the father's
married condition as it stands. Forced to participate in the

sale of his horse, the husband seems to lose not only his best friend but also a portion of his control.

Though James parrots his mother's directives to his younger brother and concerns himself with the upkeep of the chickens, his sympathies lie with his father and Scott. With the gross animal dealer MacRae as the agent of Scott's demise, one cannot help but side with the father and the horse. Scott is shed like a leaf from a tree in the fall; the change is inevitable, with a final moment of glory, and ultimately constructive. In his acceptance of loss, the father is beyond the vengeance of young David, whose parodic re-enactment of MacRae's violence neatly balances the animal losses. James nonetheless realizes that his more sensitive younger brother had something to teach him. When he realizes that the battle between his parents is less one-sided than he believed, the change in their behavior becomes more subtle and challenging to his understanding.

Students should note the smooth manner in which MacLeod works in environmental detail about the weather and the ocean. The misery of the cold rain, the weather's near-paralytic force, and the ocean's violence and continually changing surface are embedded in James's story as thematic counterpoint to the evolving action.

BOBBIE ANN MASON

Graveyard Day

(p. 964)

Mason's characters in "Graveyard Day" are ordinary small-town people whose values are shaped excessively by the media and by popular culture: Joe Murdock yearns to appear on Let's Make a Deal and idolizes the daredevil Evel Knievel; Betty and C.W. treat their trip to Sea World as a major pilgrimage; Holly names her cat after Star Trek's Mr. Spock; and Waldeen valiantly attempts to explain things to her friends in terms of Johnny Carson and Colonel Sanders. Although these preoccupations with popular culture and material goods serve as an index of shallowness, Mason does not condemn her characters; instead, she gently laughs at their foibles and sympathizes when they struggle to transcend the mundane worlds they seem to have molded for themselves.

Waldeen has occasional difficulty in sorting out the "Joe's" in her life because each successive Joe seems to be a composite character who embodies the attractive qualities of his predecessor. Joe Suitor represents the ideal of freedom and spontaneity; though he now works at a bank, his "great adventure" with Waldeen on the lake stands as an emblem of an adolescence without commitment. Joe Murdock, her first husband, possesses a similar adventurous spirit, but its unpredictable manifestations become a threat within the context of a stable, ongoing relationship. Joe McClain's surprises -- material goods and food -- are intended to enrich the texture of daily life and impress Holly and Waldeen. Yet Joe, with his somewhat affected walking stick, seems like an actor who wants to assume a role as father and husband. He is a diminished version of the other Joe's before him, and, like Mr. Spock, will become more complacent in the "nurturing" family atmosphere.

178

Betty's comment, "You must do whatever comes natural," becomes one of the story's key lines, even though Betty uses it as a rationalization for her decision not to have a child. While Joe McClain chides Waldeen for not being adventurous and Holly becomes an advocate of natural foods, Waldeen becomes the one who finally does "whatever comes natural" when she jumps into the pile of dead leaves at the conclusion of the story. Students should relate this action to her earlier reflection that "the burial plot, not a diamond ring, symbolizes the promise of marriage," and conclude that her jump indicates she is ready to "take the plunge" into marriage, though she realizes it may be her graveyard day.

ALICE MUNRO

Spelling

(p. 972)

Other stories of Flo and Rose in Munro's short story sequence
The Beggar Maid provide an illuminating background for this
one, but "Spelling" may be easily taken from its context
in the volume and read independently. Munro sensitively
depicts a domineering woman's conscious battle against
senility and the efforts of her relatives to care for her
as she begins "going off track." Always stubborn and set
in her beliefs (as the incident at the reception in Toronto
illustrates), Flo gradually becomes more difficult to veer
from her course. Her house in Hanratty embodies both her
resistance to change and her inevitable decay. The oddities
she accumulates on her porch are mementos of a rich and
varied past, and might be compared to the material goods
which Brian and Phoebe acquire as they settle into a smug
surburban existence. Rose seems to seek some middle course,
in which the quest for material success is replaced by an
ongoing concern with cultivating and using her individual
talents.

Yet while traveling and promoting the arts, Rose finds
herself going slightly "off track," as she is plagued with
self doubt and shaken by periodic bouts of guilt about
forsaking her mother. Rose is ready to live peacefully in
her childhood home and lose herself in the role of Flo's
nursemaid/companion, but Flo will not allow her any such
easy reconciliation. Students might compare this behavior
with Flo's letter to Rose about baring her breast in the
play and observe Flo's consistency in undercutting her
daughter's complacency. In spite of her arthritis and
mental lapses, Flo attempts to maintain her dignity and

180

upset Rose's well-laid plans. Rose's ambivalence about
her scheme to place Flo in a nursing home manifests itself
in her dream of a caged Flo, spelling grandly like the old
woman Rose has just seen at the home.

For this woman, spelling seems to be her last connection
with the outside world and a final grasp on maintaining her
senses. Yet Rose also recognizes that with the inner vision
of senility, the letters may also serve as a "parade of
private visitors," full of wonder that only a person who
has retreated into her memories may witness. Munro's story
should produce some discussion of senility, nursing homes,
and care of the aged, using Flo's carefully depicted character
as the touchstone. The story's conclusion, marked by both
comic banter and obvious signs of Flo's retreat into memory,
portrays an equilibrium that seems static in contrast to
the conflict a more vital Flo could generate. The wig
which should evoke memories of the trouble she caused Rose
in Toronto now resembles "a dead squirrel" -- a memento
that has lost its vital connection to shared memory.

TIM O'BRIEN

Going After Cacciato

(p. 982)

"Going After Cacciato" contains strong thematic and stylistic
echoes of Hemingway's A Farewell to Arms. Like Fredrick
Henry, Cacciato abandons a war which has lost its meaning
and attempts to establish a separate peace. O'Brien also
uses rain to establish a mood of misery and suffering in a
style reminiscent of the opening of Hemingway's novel.
However, in O'Brien's story the significance of the rain
shifts as the scene changes: when the squad leaves camp
for the mountains, the rain is described poetically ("glue
that stuck the sky to the land"); later, as the squad sits
beneath a ledge in Cacciato's abandoned camp, the rain
seems peaceful. By the end of the story, the rain is
neither symbolic nor melancholy; it becomes "simple rain,"
just as the war itself loses its symbolic significance for
the soldiers and promotes apathy among them.

For the lieutenant suffering from dysentery, the war
in Vietnam lacks the heroic flavor of the Korean conflict,
but his persistence in going after Cacciato arises from his
belief that "it's still a war." He believes that certain
wartime codes and ethics must still be observed in order to
keep the horror and absurdity of this war from overtaking
himself and those under his command. Cacciato thus becomes
"the enemy" to be hunted because he has rebelled against
this order. His wild plan to walk 6800 miles to Paris, in
comparison to the self-inflicted injuries of fellow squad
members Vaught and Nystrom, at first seem irrational but
slightly less absurd; when we find out that Cacciato needs
only to cross the Vietnam border to be free, the plan seems

to possess more method than madness. After all, the other
missing squad members mentioned early in the story have all
been killed; Cacciato may not be leaving with all his
senses, but he hopes to take with him his life.

Whether Cacciato is indeed "dumb" should provide a
focus for discussion. Paul Berlin, whose consciousness the
narrator enters most frequently, prefers to see him as
unfinished. Cacciato's foolish scheme, his flapping arms,
and persistent smile seem to indicate some mental imbalance,
but this characteristic serves him well in battle and
fosters a single-mindedness that may bring success to his
plan to go AWOL. He is cagey enough to set a trap which
will frighten and warn, but not kill, his pursuers, even
after he has shed a considerable amount of his gear and
equipment. Most of Cacciato's squad members pity and
sympathize with him, and seem inclined to let him go, though
the trap changes at least one person's attitude. In the
end, the squad does follow the lieutenant's orders, yet
Berlin's behavior reveals their hope that the mission fail;
his final "Go" seems to be urging and cheering Cacciato in
his futile but admirable farewell to arms.

CYNTHIA OZICK ====

The Shawl

(p. 996)

William Abrahams, who awarded Ozick's story First Prize in
Prize Stories: The O'Henry Awards 1981, calls it a "parable
of the Holocaust . . . As the facts recede into history and
become the premise of scholars, art -- as it expresses
itself in 'The Shawl' -- will endure; not, if you like, a
'story,' but a 'memory' to haunt whoever reads it."
Discussion of Ozick's powerful and evocative story might
focus on how art -- especially a brief story such as this
one -- can bring historical circumstances to life by
portraying the emotions behind them. Ozick makes us aware
of the Holocaust setting without explicit mention of Nazis
or the concentration camp. Instead, she uses words and
images intimately associated with the Holocaust to set the
scene: the barracks, the term "Aryan," the roll-call arena,
bitter smoke, goblet-shaped helmets, black boots, and an
electrified fence. Complementing these realistic details
are those whose effect derives from Ozick's skillful use of
figurative language: Rosa'a dried breasts, for example,
are like a "dead volcano," and Magda's lone tooth resembles
"an elfin tombstone." Amid these and other images of death,
students might feel that the lyric imagery of the final
scene is out of place. This imagery only serves to augment
the harsh and hopeless plight of the doomed prisoners. When
the guard tosses Magda into the electrified fence, his
action becomes even more horrible because of the abrupt end
of her butterfly-like flight.
     Throughout the ordeal, Rosa's shawl works a type of
magic. As Magda's substitute for nourishment, it promotes
the silence that guarantees her continued secret existence,

184

though it also breeds jealousy in Stella. At the end of the story, the shawl also saves Rosa'a life, stopping up the scream of pain that would cause the guards to shoot her. For both Magda and her mother, silence guarantees repressed survival, while verbal expression may produce immediate death. The vitality of both Ozick's characters and the story itself resides beneath the surface, and becomes all the more powerful as a result.

GRACE PALEY

The Used-Boy Raisers

(p. 1000)

In Paley's volume <u>The Little Disturbances of Man</u>, "The Used-Boy Raisers" is the first of "Two Short Sad Stories from a Long and Happy Life." Although the situation sketched in Paley's story is less than ideal, we might wonder whether this is indeed a sad story, at least from the narrator's point of view. Faith herself does little to create an impression of sadness; she seems curiously aloof from the little disturbances of man as her husbands "set off in pride on paths which are not my concern" at the story's conclusion.

Her destiny, Faith believes, is "to be, until my expiration date, laughingly the servant of man," yet her re-marriage to Pallid has overtones of surrender and submission which may not lead to a long and happy life. At her worst, Faith seems resigned and ineffectual; at best, she seems content and able to exercise some control over her household domain. She is devoted to Richard and Tonto, the "used-boys" of the title, who have been transferred from one raiser to the next, as a used car is transferred from one owner to the next. Their confusion over who their "real father" is near the end of the story should indicate that they have not made the transition as smoothly as their imperturbable mother.

At first glance, the allegorical naming of the characters might seem identical to Hawthorne's technique in "Young Goodman Brown." Livid and Pallid both manifest the dominant qualitites their names indicate, but Faith's name is perhaps somewhat ironic since she does not sustain any strong beliefs from her Jewish heritage and seems content to express her faith in embroidered religious samplers. Paley's Faith resembles Hawthorne's character as she is initially portrayed in his famous story, but bears little resemblance to the Faith whom Goodman Brown envisions at the gathering in the forest.

Paley uses the explicit similarity to Hawthorne's allegory about shaken religious beliefs to establish her story as a modern morality play about the inadequacy of domestic life in a less religious-centered society. Thus, the long discussion about religion is not tangential matter but rather essential background for these otherwise flat characters. Livid is vehemently opposed to religion as a "grotto of deception," while Pallid meekly asserts religion's enduring influence for modern freethinkers who hear church bells peal from afar. Faith's diluted Jewish heritage and her belief in the Diaspora represent another variety of the loss of religious security. In the end, material security seems to be the predominant struggle of Paley's characters.

Students may find the lack of quotation marks extremely confusing, but should be encouraged to explore the effects of this technique, especially the flat, even tone which results from giving equal weight to dialogue, description, and reflection.

Dillinger in Hollywood

(p. 1005)

Sayles is better known as a scriptwriter and film director, so it should be no surprise that "Dillinger in Hollywood" is filled with allusions to famous film heroes and directors. Yet this story is less concerned with the Hollywood establishment than with those who have lived on the periphery of its glamor and have now begun the "down cycle," as Casey terms it. Both Hollywood and the nursing home for its aging outsiders are filled with those whose primary concern is creating illusions. The nursing home residents have been through Hollywood's cycle and attempted to build their lives around its dreams; now they fabricate glorious pasts in their struggles to maintain some hold on dignity as age and faded dreams overtake them.

The narrator is also one who has been through Hollywood's cycle; after a fall from a horse ends his career as a stuntman, he drifts into "the geriatric game." His imagination has been permanently tinged by Hollywood as well, but he manages to maintain a healthy sense of humor to insulate himself from the tragedy of kindred wash-outs from Hollywood. His narration is punctuated with brief explanations that create a sense of the absurd (e.g., "Roscoe had been in The Wizard of Oz as a Munchkin and was a very deep thinker. He reads the kind of science-fiction books that don't have girls in loincloths on the cover.") Despite his comparison of geriatrics with horses and the use of such labels as "vegematics" for patients who can no longer take care of themselves, we sense his unspoken sympathy, which emerges most strongly during Casey's final attempt "to be somebody."

Casey's claim that he "used to be John Dillinger" seems at first to be a response to Spurs Tatum's obvious fabrication or a privately-held delusion that has recently surfaced. Tatum's boasts about his exploits as a stuntman, the narrator notes, might have some connection to real events, but Casey's former role seems pure fiction until the narrator senses the force of his conviction and discovers that he lacks a recorded past before 1937. The narrator's tenative suspension of disbelief, arising in part from sympathy, might be compared to Nora's unquestioning acceptance of Casey as Dillinger. A failed actress, she becomes a collaborator in his fiction, reinforcing his illusion with her mild hero-worship. Casey's last words -- "I used to be somebody" -- illustrate that his Dillinger story is his final attempt to maintain dignity in the face of his imminent decline. According to Casey, he (as Dillinger) has cheated death by having a double killed and assuming another identity. Dillinger, a media rather than a movie "hero," is nonetheless an appropriate choice for a geriatric's glamorous past. Legend portrays him as a sexually potent outlaw who continually defied fate; killed while leaving a movie, Dillinger spent his last hours immersed in the illusions of the screen, just as the geriatrics spend the last cycle of their lives in illusions of their own making.

LYNNE SHARON SCHWARTZ ≣

Rough Strife

(p. 1014)

Students are asked to read Andrew Marvell's "To His Coy
Mistress" as a point of comparison. While Marvell's poem
is a suitor's invitation to "sport," Schwartz's story
portrays the possible aftermath of such a courtship:
conception, pregnancy, and childbirth. Marvell's speaker
urges his reluctant mistress to "tear our pleasures with
rough strife," but rough strife in this story is an ongoing
state of conflict between the expectant couple. The story's
seasonal time frame loosely reflects the course of events:
the child is conceived during the resurgent passion of
Indian summer; winter corresponds to the darkest, most self-
absorbed stage of Caroline's pregnancy; spring brings a
rebirth to the passions which have lain dormant and produces
constructive conflict; and the child is born during summer's
fullness.
    Both Caroline and Ivan are portrayed realistically,
with weaknesses as well as strengths, both of which emerge
sporadically during the pregnancy, almost in an alternating
pattern. When Caroline finally summons her will, Ivan's
seems to diminish. Caroline's lethargy and fears increase
as she focuses more intently on the changes occurring within
her. Students might note that during her pregnancy she
smokes and drinks alcohol, neither of which is condoned by
most physicians. Overall, however, she seems to be
sympathetically portrayed as a woman who bravely copes with
the physical and emotional turbulence of her first pregnancy.
Ivan may be somewhat less favorably portrayed, but only
because we occasionally see him from Caroline's point of
view and never view Caroline from his. Ivan's initial

190

doting fondness cannot withstand his insistent doubts about and fear of fatherhood; as Caroline reaches the final stages of her pregnancy, he retreats into sullen indifference, but emerges at the end to assist in the natural childbirth.

The couple seems at its worst when the relationship assumes the character of a passive reconciliation. William Blake's concept of marriage as a dynamic and progressive war between contrary states may be a useful related idea to introduce here. The moments of rough strife which erupt periodically between Caroline and Ivan arouse them from their torpor and help them discover more creative ways to combat their problems as well as each other. Caroline's question about the weather after the child is born marks her emergence from her concentration on the life within. Significantly, the weather outside indicates the co-existence of contrary states that will continue to mark the couple's new life.

ELIZABETH SPENCER

The Girl Who Loved Horses

(p. 1027)

A lusty eater and drinker and a lover of fast horses,
Deborah is unmistakably a character who seeks to burn
with a hard, gem-like flame; in the first scene, her near
oneness with the horse she rides signals a desire to lose
herself in intense, passionate moments. Emma, her mother,
serves as a powerless normative character who wants her
daughter to have a family and who ineffectually opposes
having her historic farm turned into a stable. Deborah's
animal passions, however, must run their course before she
accedes of her own will to her mother's desires. Her
dormant passions have been re-awakened by Clyde, whose
masculinity and interest in horses evoke Deborah's memory
of the drumming hoofs and wild rides of her childhood.
Clyde is relatively undeveloped as a character; at first he
and Deborah seem to be complementary, but when he harnesses
her pleasure in horses for the horse breeding and showing
business, the nature of their passions changes. Deborah
physically blossoms under Clyde's rein, but their fiery
relationship cools as the business prospers.
   The kinship Deborah recognizes between herself and the
hired man is much more sinister. He represents the darker
side of passion, but Deborah is both attracted to and
repelled by "the poor-man's Clyde" whose animal-like nature
is more elemental than her own. As she watches her effect
on him, Deborah's sense of superiority and her pity for
animals change to a realization that her power and her
expressive use of animals as outlets for her passion have
their limits. Spencer's study of Deborah's secret shame
for her attraction might lead some students to misread the

rape scene. Deborah's attraction to the hired man arises from her perception of a kindred but baser passion in him; she senses his animal helplessness and his power, but does not desire him sexually. She keeps the attempted rape secret not because she feels responsible for it but because she considers her battle with the hired man to be a private war of wills that she must win without Clyde's aid or pity.

Combined with her growing estrangement from Clyde, this incident affects Deborah's skill in breaking wild horses. Her fear manifests itself in an increased awareness of the danger of her profession and in nightmares of being trampled. Until she meets and defeats her assailant again, Deborah is unable to use her strength to assert herself against Clyde. The hired man becomes the last animal whose spirit she will break. Although Deborah boldly wins the contest of wills so completely that she feels no need to shoot him, her victory becomes tainted by the image of his "worthless" eyes, which seem to reflect that part of herself which has been tamed in the process. The stylistic change in the abduction scene illustrates a Deborah depending less on instinctual reaction than on a more reflective, self-conscious process of thought. Although she becomes the girl who <u>loved</u> horses, Deborah does not abandon her passion for existence when she ceases to ride; she merely seeks other outlets for that passion and regains some measure of her lost control.

Home and Native Land

(p. 1039)

Virgo's story very briefly sketches a Canadian subculture in disintegration. As in a mystery story, we must take note of small details and puzzle out exactly what the motives of the characters are. While we see Ron's restlessness, the reasons for his disturbed spirit are far from evident. His long hair and worn city clothes, as well as the term he has spent in prison, indicate some separation from the village and its traditional ways. His mental distance from his home and native land promotes an easy camaraderie with the two outsiders and makes it easier for him to assist them with their grave-robbing in return for what we assume to be drugs.

Yet because the events are seen through his brother's consciousness, it is difficult to dismiss Ron as a malcontent and a renegade. Dickie's admiration for and devotion to Ron persist in spite of his brother's behavior. In addition, the symbolic connection between Ron and the eagle reinforces this admiration; yet it should be noted that the eagle in this story is both majestic and predatory. Initially, the eagle is beseiged by two gulls as it drags a beached horseshoe crab out of the tide, just as Ron is approached by the two strangers. When he joins the two men in their journey to the burial ground, these three birds fly away together; both Ron and the eagle in this case diminish in stature. Finally, the eagle bracelet which Ron wears upon his return links him with the eagle and past tribal glory, but its smell of death clearly taints this relic of nobility and proud spirit.

While Ron joins in the plundering without qualms,
Dickie's more sensitive spirit recoils from the desecration
of the traditional burial ground; the sea-bird's shriek
becomes in his mind the equivalent of a screeching coffin
lid. His attachment to the traditonal culture finally
conflicts with his reverence of Ron, who appears more like
a puppet of the two outsiders as the "sea mirage" lifts
from Dickie's eyes. The final scene on the island confirms
Dickie's worst fears (as well as our own); confronting the
realistic detail of the grave-robbing, we discover the low
point to which Ron has descended. Dickie is not as worried
about tribal superstitions as he is about the society's
inability to bury its recent dead safely, without disturbance
of the cultural artifacts which are gradually being laid to
rest with them.

Roselily

(p. 1043)

The central drama of Walker's story occurs in the main
character's consciousness as she responds to specific words
and phrases of the traditional wedding ceremony. In this
manner, Roselily progressively reveals her troubled past,
her dissatisfaction with her present life in the rural
community of her birth, and her ambivalent expectations for
the future. Her reflections are generally ironic and self-
questioning, often bitterly so. She seems painfully aware
that her marriage is no more than a means of escape from a
stagnant situation and that her life in the city will at
best be one of mixed blessings. Though she will gain
security and certain material advantages, she will be
shackled to a religion and a social role which constrict
rather than liberate her vital and imaginative character.
     Roselily's doubts about the applicability of
traditional values are only part of the opposition sketched
between herself and her new husband. While the easy-going
Roselily has a rural Christian background, her husband is
a stern Black Muslim from Chicago who promises a well-
ordered and comfortable existence. Roselily seems an
unlikely candidate for a traditional role as a suburban
housewife, and the dominant colors of her future--gray and
black--provide a sense of foreboding. Roselily's name
suggests that her dominant qualities are embodied by the
traditional colors of love and vitality; her husband's
severe black suit and the cinders of Chicago loom darkly
in her future. Her abundant use of simile and metaphor
likewise indicates the imaginative vitality that will
persist behind her outward submission; she will attempt to

196

cling to her present identity even though she adopts a new
social role.

The Farm

(p. 1047)

The anecdote about the alligator with which "The Farm"
opens illustrates that little in a short story is superfluous
and that foreshadowing is often only recognized in retrospect.
The alligator's killing of the child provides an ironic
parallel to Sarah's accidental killing of Stevie Bettencourt.
While the alligator is shot as a potential danger, Sarah is
"protected" by her husband Tommy in the insulated shelter of
their restored country house. The anecdote might also relate
to Genevieve's subtle intrusion into Sarah's life; like the
alligator, Genevieve may be a "robber" who wants to share
Sarah's child to compensate for the loss of her own. Sarah's
initial resistance to her neighbor's overtures will, as the
omniscient narrator notes, give way. Genevieve's revelations
about the original state of the restored house--its lobster
tank and the whale bones buried in the garden--force Sarah to
see beyond the surface of things. Her "adulterous feelings"
arise because she feels unfaithful to Tommy in threatening
the fragile illusion he has created. In the end, she does
not perceive herself as Genevieve's victim but believes that
some justice has been accomplished.

Sarah seems to believe that her alcoholism can provide
her with great insight into the world around her, while her
periods of abstinence produce a "great and impenetrable
silence." The causes of her alcoholism are never made
explicit, but it seems to grow out of the lifestyle she and
Tommy adopt. Her drinking problem spirals so far out of
control that she identifies people by what they serve to
drink at parties and becomes careless enough to run over a
similarly-dazed young boy. Whether Sarah is intoxicated or

sober, however, her perceptions are portrayed as somewhat surreal; she is a numbed outsider unable to comprehend her surroundings. Yet her insights into Genevieve's motives and the concluding statement about robbers demonstrate that reality is beginning to penetrate her defenses.

Stevie's phrase for "dead"--"bought the farm"--gains highly ironic implications when Tommy announces that he is considering buying yet another old farm to restore. Tommy's culpability for Sarah's condition cannot be minimized, as he leads another existence in the city while keeping Sarah down on the farm. Her immersion in household chores becomes a type of living death from which Genevieve might force her to emerge. The "safety" of yet another farm would kill whatever chances for rebirth she has by taking away her chance to establish some roots and combat her isolation.